EXPRESSIONS *of* ONENESS

EXPRESSIONS *of* ONENESS

MARRIAGE

CHILD-RAISING

SPIRITUAL COMMUNITY

as PRIMARY

SOUL RELATIONSHIPS

jean shorter

as inspired by the Akashic Records

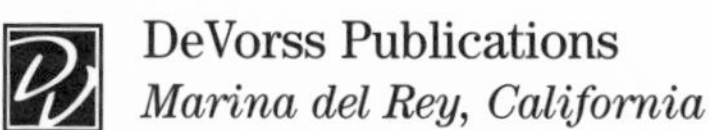

DeVorss Publications
Marina del Rey, California

Expressions of Oneness

Authorization to use the lines from *The Propet,* by Kahlil Gibran, quoted on pp. 71 and 115 was also granted by the Gibran National Committe, P.O. Box 116-5487, Beirut, Lebanon;
Fax (+961-1)396916; E-mail: k.gibran@cybenia.net lb.

ISBN: 0-87516-736-5
Library of Congress Catalog Card Number: 00-130621

DeVorss & Company, Publisher
Box 550
Marina del Rey CA 90294-0550

Printed in the United States of America

This book is dedicated to the children—
all the children
who are leading us in light and love.
As well, it is dedicated to my partner, Ces,
in whom the eternal child is most vibrant and alive.

C O N T E N T S

Book Two

Preparing the Way

Teachings on Our Sacred Contract with Children

Book Three

Spiritual Community

The Transformation of the World through Soul Purpose

PREFACE

At this time in our human history, there are many messages and many messengers whose purpose is, as it would appear to be, to enable and assist every one of us in coming to terms with a great and far-reaching transformation of consciousness.

These teachings, which are the result of innumerable Akashic Record readings, are likewise intended to be of help to any who are seeking a more enlightened view of the central relationships in their lives and, indeed, the soul wisdom that guides each of these relationships.

For it is the soul that seeks relationship. It is the soul that recognizes our connection to all life. And so these teachings are offered that they may inspire a greater understanding, a greater wisdom for any who would reclaim the sacred purpose of marriage, honor the sacred contract we all have with the children of the world or discover the profound and purposeful support of true community.

For all these reasons and more, the soul of humanity—the world soul, of which each one of our souls is a part—is seeking recognition, a realization of what has often been called the Christ consciousness within.

This is to say that unity and peace and a great sharing of life's resources shall come into being in the New Age that is being born. And, to the extent that one has the ability to thus embrace what is unfolding for the good of all mankind, these teachings come as a support, an inspiration, indeed, a reason to live in greater awareness of all that we are being asked and being invited to make real in our lives and in the world.

For such is the soul dream—no matter what else we are here to do, it is the deep desire of everyone to live in greater harmony, to play a part in this new world that is being born. Or we wouldn't be here. Such is the teaching of the Masters—those who have been the great source of wisdom through the ages.

That new teachings come now in order to assist us is but a part of the plan. For each and every one of us has much to give. And, in this, as in everything, we are supported in light and love. Always.

It is, for me, both an honor and a privilege to make these teachings available to you. And it is my hope that you will find they resonate with the truth of your own heart, whoever you are.

Take from them what you will. And, together, may we have the good fortune to see the new world, which is, as yet, in the making. May these teachings give you every hope and every cause for renewing the particular dream you carry within you. Nothing is more fulfilling—something I have come to know well, as this work has long been my dream.

ACKNOWLEDGMENTS

I wish to thank Linda Howe for her unfailing support of this work and her contribution to my understanding of these teachings. I wish to thank Arthur Vergara for his support and his constant patience with me throughout the entire process. Likewise, I thank Gary Peattie for his support and willingness to explore alternatives. Special thanks to Don Brown for his generous spirit and expert advice. I also wish to express my deepest gratitude to my mother, Marjorie, who always, always encouraged me to write, and to my husband, Ces, who supported my efforts even when he didn't realize he was doing so. Love and thanks to you all.

Book One

THE SACRED MARRIAGE

Teachings on the Soul Dimension of Life Partnership

Introduction

Relationships are sacred. They are God's way of leading us to Him through another. It is by seeing God in another, seeing the divine spirit that works in and through them, that we connect with the divine spirit in ourselves and in others outside the one-to-one committed relationship.

It is the center of a circle, a marriage. A circle that holds two, and yet is ever widening its arc, ever growing towards the ultimate inclusion of All That Is. For this reason are two people joined in spirit. And only for this reason.

You may think otherwise—the illusions of romantic love are many. But in truth, they serve only to facilitate the joining of two hearts for a far higher purpose. And that has always been so. It is why marriage is considered a sacrament. It is why people speak of marriage as spiritual partnership today.

Teachings about the nature and challenges of such a union are offered here to any that would find use for them, to any seeking guidance on this path. They are offered in answer to a great desire on the part of many of you to be more conscious in relating, in learning what your partners, as teachers, are here to offer you in this life and what you, in turn, have to give.

These teachings are also offered as a means of support for those who find themselves living in a time when partnerships are all too easily dissolved, when the sacred dimension of marriage is often overlooked, when the real purpose for which two people come together is so easily lost sight of amid the everyday difficulties and distractions of modern life—which isn't nearly as evolved as people would like to think.

In some ways, much has been lost. Things which were once understood, which were taken to heart in simpler times, are now the province only of those who take great pains to seek them out, to uncover the real reason couples are drawn to one another again and again, despite all manner of suffering that is involved.

And people do suffer. For it is human nature to resist the path to wholeness, the path to awareness of our divine selves. And it is far easier to blame our partners for any pain, any discomfort, any confusion this resistance creates.

A more enlightened perspective is offered here as a way of helping you to see that what causes you the most pain with that person you are most vulnerable to is exactly where your life lesson is. And, yes, until one opens to the lesson and lets go of resistance, the lesson will surface again and again and again. In other words, you may often feel that your partner is making you crazy—but, alas, it is you, yourself.

Your partner is the willing soul with whom you have an agreement to work out this lesson. The many disguises your partner may appear in—from the sweetest man or woman on earth to, perhaps,a raving lunatic—is a co-creation between the two of you which mirrors what you need to look at, what you need to examine sincerely within yourself, within your own being.

Once this is understood (by the way, there is much in mythology to shed light on this), people are able to stop punishing each other, to move past their particular day-to-day drama into a state of grace.

Openness and a humble approach to that which is one's highest growth, and a willingness not to know, but be shown the way, brings forth untold blessings. (Yes, blessings—an archaic notion to many, but real just the same.) Blessings which not only help an individual to grow more quickly and with far less pain, but which bring great joy to your sacred union. In other words, the door to happiness is precisely where your pain is.

These things are not much spoken of today. Instead people scrutinize a partner to learn if they can meet the (usually neurotic) needs of the personality—unaware they are even doing this. Or quite reluctant to admit it. Worse, some callously assert that this is reasonable or worthwhile, when it is, indeed, foolishness.

Reclaiming the sacred purpose of monogamous union is as important as any work we would do. As Rainer Maria Rilke said:

> *For one human being to love another human being: that is perhaps the most difficult task that has been entrusted to us, the ultimate task, the final test and proof, the work for which all other work is merely preparation.**

It is nothing less than coming to know God, coming face to face with God's manifestation in yourselves and in each other. Human beings, after all, come to love—love for all of humanity—with but one other person at a time.

Which is not to say you love only one, but that the process of opening the heart, the act of sharing your soul completely with another, is how you come to know, the way in which you connect with, the way in which you experience the divine creator within yourself and in us all—if not for the first time, in a very powerful way. The divine source whom you have always been a part of, though you have forgotten this truth.

These teachings are a reminder. They are meant for those who seek to honor one another, who seek to know God by whatever name you choose. The knowing is more important than the naming. The knowing is your only true path.

Blessed are those who would love one another, for in their open hearts they will find God. And in finding God, they will find joy beyond measure.

Or, as Rumi might have put it: The Beloved and I are one. And yet we dance.

* From *Letters to a Young Poet,* by Rainer Maria Rilke, translated by Stephen Mitchell (N. Y.: Vintage Books, a division of Random House, 1984), p. 68.

One

Allow for the Possibility of Guidance

MARRIAGE IS not the only sacred union. But it is the most prevalent way in which individuals in modern society encounter the Divine. And so these teachings are offered, are extended to those who would learn from them, in order that they may have a great impact on consciousness in the world today—a far greater impact than anyone might imagine.

For though there are many spiritual teachings being channeled at this time, a great many of you are most of all preoccupied with your romantic lives. It is very human to feel this way. Nevertheless, this is not the only task at hand. And this business of romance is so much more than it appears to be.

Marriage comes from the Latin word *maritare*—the union of man and woman through the Goddess Mari. It means surrendering to another human being as a way of opening one's heart to God, the Goddess, the Divine Creator.

It is this quality of surrender that is particularly difficult, particularly challenging for men and women who see themselves as masters of the universe or as separate, self-reliant beings with no need for anyone else, if truth be told.

This is one of the greatest illusions of all—the illusion of separateness. As though anything in the Universe could be said to exist in solitariness, let alone a man or a woman. You are connected to all life, whether you know it or not. This is no mere slogan for the purpose of bumper stickers or causes.

This is reality. This is the inescapable truth, a truth you will come to know through the experience of union with your partner—one of your own choosing with whom you have a soul agreement. And only one partner in your lifetime.

For though you may know many partners in many lives before you are complete in the knowledge that you are one with God, it is profoundly difficult for one to make the journey home, to make the passages of soul that are required for you to become conscious of being one with the Divine Creator, when relating to more than one person at a time. (Ask any parent how difficult it is to stay conscious while juggling a marriage, a family, a career.)

So you choose one person with whom you have an agreement, a soul agreement, to consider marriage. And there are often many to choose from. The idea that a person has but one soul mate is quite false. Think how dull things would be lifetime after lifetime.

No, each person comes into this world with many agreements. A choice is made. Or not. (Yes, there are those whom you choose not to fulfill your agreements with, for one reason or another.) But once you choose, a process is set in motion that doesn't stop until it is complete. Until each person has come to see that the Beloved is really the Divine and that they, themselves, are no different.

This is what makes divorce a sticky subject. It is a choice you have, to be sure. But it merely postpones the lessons the two of you have come into the world to give one another.

In rare circumstances, divorce may be the best choice available to a person in violent or life-threatening circumstances. But more often than not it is, instead, a matter of so-called convenience. (As if postponing the lessons to life times hence were in any way convenient. But so be it.)

On the other hand, if one chooses to see a higher purpose at work in their relationship, they are better able to deal with the challenges that occur. It is the case that people who see the divine process at work in each other are more forgiving of themselves and each other. It is the case that people who accept that a higher force is guiding them to what their souls long for are people who create enduring love—a love that grows beyond them in every way. Beyond the two of them to parents, children and extended families. Beyond this lifetime. And beyond this world.

So how do you come to see all this in another? It's easy. It's given to you. It's part of the initial drawing together, the attraction, the pull between souls.

Losing this vision—not acquiring it—is the problem human beings face. And it is only by learning to maintain this soul vision that one comes to grace. Through grace, blessings are manifest continually.

Blessings that will show you exactly what it is that you need to learn.

Think how often you may have stormed away in anger when you and your spouse have disagreed. This was no less than turning your back on a blessing that was meant for you. And only you.

It is intervention only—conscious intervention by you, yourself—that can change this. And that is not easy to do. Because your ego is almost always in the way.

Yet if you care for another as much as you care for yourself (and most of you don't regard yourselves nearly as well as you think you do), you must ask yourself: "If there is a blessing here, why would I keep that from anyone, even me?"

Catch yourself in such moments. Breathe. Ask yourself this simple question. Expect blessings and you shall receive them.

Make this your habit, not recriminations. Make this your goal. And forgive yourself if you can't always do it. But give yourself to this task with all sincerity and your love will grow. Your soul vision will increase, not fade away. Your union will truly be what it was always intended to be. A profound gift of love. A high calling. Safe passage home.

That is the first lesson we have to give. Accomplish this and you will do more than you ever thought possible in your soap opera world.

In wise love each divines the high secret self of the other, and, refusing to believe in mere daily self, creates a mirror where the lover or the beloved sees an image to copy in daily life.

W. B. Yeats

Two

The Importance of Soul Vision

SOUL VISION IS what you could call "looking through the eyes of love," as the song says. It means seeing another person in a way one doesn't normally see them. It's a glimpse of the soul, not merely the physical being before you.

This is what allows two people to come together, to commit their lives and their hearts to one another. But people have difficulty sustaining this soul vision over time.

The answer lies in renewing it now and then, versus the impossible task of seeing in this way at all times, in every moment of day-to-day life.

Soul vision is a powerful and, to a large degree, self-sustaining phenomenon. It doesn't take much to keep it going. But it does require an alertness to, an awareness of, the subtle signs that tell you when it's beginning to wane.

When you find yourself impatient with your partner or struggling to be understood, when you find yourself having to be right about something, it is usually a sign that you need a renewal of soul.

There are a million ways to do this. Some involve quiet time for you and your partner, perhaps in a nature setting that restores your sense of wonder. Others are quite solitary, involving time out from life's daily demands and frustrations.

No matter which you choose at any given time, consider it an opportunity to ask yourself, to contemplate with the heart and not the head, "Who is it I am being asked to become?" "What is this relationship asking of me and what, if anything, prevents me from answering the call?"

Ask for guidance, invoke the god self within (this is the power of prayer) and your soul will, indeed, reveal itself to you. You will come to see where it is you must be willing to go, who it is you must become in order to create a relationship that truly nourishes your authentic soul self and that of your partner.

This kind of renewal amounts to taking a cooling off period *before* an argument ensues. It's nurturing the soul so as to avoid the argument, if you will. The argument itself is like an alarm that goes off—then you really know something's wrong. But if you see the signs sooner, it's possible to work out your differences without a fight.

Doing these things that nurture your soul also enables you to see another's soul process, to appreciate their struggle to grow into awareness. Renewing your soul gives you the compassion to forgive your differences. And it helps you to realize that most of what people go through isn't directed at you personally, it's just what they go through.

There is a kind of detachment in all this that is not unlike Buddhist philosophy. A more detached view allows grace to flow. And where grace flows there is effortless compassion and love.

When we stop insisting that someone else be what we want them to be or do what we want them to do and just let them be who they are at any given moment, all things are possible. We may even find we get what we want when we're not so insistent—that, whatever it is, it's freely given when forgiveness or appreciation is the intention and not bending another's will.

Yes, intention is the critical element here. Intention is always felt, whether it is conscious or not, let alone spoken. And, quite often, words are actually used to deny one's true intention.

Consider the feeling we have of knowing when someone is lying, for example. The feeling of their intention is in conflict with the words we hear. And this inconsistency prevents us from accepting their words. This is one of the ways the wisdom of the body works. The body interprets the energy of intention, the mind interprets the words. When the two are at odds, you have a suspension of belief.

Think on this, think how many times each of you has been on one side or the other. This knowing, this feeling in the gut, is quite unmistakable.

When our intention is forgiveness or understanding or compassion, on the other hand, we transcend our circumstances and move to a place of possibility. This shift, as people call it, is absolutely necessary in moving forward on any problem or issue you have with another human being.

In fact, until you are in this place of possibility,

until this shift occurs, you are wasting your breath if you try to tackle any serious issues. It would be better to keep things light, to do things you enjoy, or take a walk in the woods alone and renew your own spirit than to take up any serious discussions with your partner. And yet this is precisely when people want most to resolve whatever it is that's bothering them.

This is the nature of the soap opera. You're seeking relief. You want to feel better fast. But often you're choosing the worst possible moment to do it.

The result is usually an escalation of conflict. And an escalation of conflict is definitely not something to be encouraged. There is all manner of damage done when conflict erupts—damage which is never entirely undone in most cases, though healing is always possible.

The healing process, however, is most often not allowed to complete itself. Conflicts continually arise that disrupt the healing process and you are, in a sense, starting over each time. (You could learn something from animals that retreat to lick their wounds and recover before venturing out into the world again.)

There are endless reasons to renew your soul and maintain a soul vision of your partner. For one thing, it allows you to keep your intentions honorable. When your intentions are honorable and good, and not manipulative in any way, it is much easier to resolve differences. And when differences are resolved easily, it's actually far more likely that the two of you can come to respect, appreciate and love them. For differences not only contribute greatly to growth, they make life far more interesting than it would be if you had only yourself to consider.

Differences between people are akin to diversity in a healthy ecosystem. They are enlivening, enriching, and, at times, challenging. But there isn't one of you who can live without challenge. It is a fundamental aspect of human life, of any biological organism, of any organic process. And it is true for soul growth as well. Challenge is what pulls you forward into another state of being, over and over again. Unless it is resisted.

Resistance demands more than its share of energy from any dynamic system, however. It can even drain the most fundamental energy a system devotes to maintaining itself. And that's when you have a breakdown of the system. Collapse. Dissolution. And regression to a lower state.

Resistance—the willful avoidance of expansion and growth and the desire to control a process that is outside of the control of the personality—is the reason people suffer so in relationships.

Give it up. Allow. Allow. Allow. Embrace your challenges. Love those that bring them to you, for, indeed, they are God's messengers. They are your soul teachers. They reveal yourself to you. Always.

Three

Letting Go Is Most Important When It's Hardest to Do.

ALL MARRIAGES ARE difficult. And the truth is that very few of you are really prepared for this. There is even an idea in the culture that when a relationship is working, something is wrong. There is an expression, "Loving someone shouldn't be so hard," and other variations on this notion. Nothing could be further from the truth. Not because love has to be hard, but because you make it so.

If everyone were totally free of resistance, totally open to growth and totally willing to face themselves as revealed in another, love would be an effortless thing. But no one can live up to that.

So to think a relationship should be easier than it proves to be is really not a good reason to end it. We would even say that when it's particularly difficult and challenging is when you have the most to learn, the most to gain, in terms of your own growth and development.

Yet this is precisely the point where things break down. If you see no higher purpose to your relationship, it's easy to understand why. If all you acknowledge is pain and problems, with no redeeming quality to any of it, you can't see a reason to go on. And you find it very hard to forgive.

If you do, however, know your partner to be your best teacher, one who is showing you the way home—though it may not look like that at all—you will have more courage, more willingness to overcome the difficulties that are to be found in any relationship. (Including the next one you find yourself in, if you do decide to call it quits.)

Couples who share this view can do much to support each other in this process of growth too.In fact, the more you learn about other people's difficulties in relationship, the less alone you feel, the more likely you are to want to own your own issues (which may not seem so bad after all), and the more you'll be able to laugh at yourselves and the predicaments you find yourselves in over and over again.

At times, you will, indeed, see patterns along gender lines. Other times, not. At times, you'll realize your own ability to see another's mistake is because it's an issue for you too. And, eventually, you'll realize how much couples recycle the very same stuff. It may look like a different issue on the surface, but when you get right down to it, it's an issue they've struggled with a thousand times before. (A lesson is experienced again and again to be learned, remember?)

Take, for example, the issue of jealousy. Some people claim to be jealous types, others not. But if they really examine the subject, they're more likely to find they're both jealous types—but it manifests differently. They're jealous over different things. So if these two people are in a relationship together, any problems or difficulties around the issue of jealousy are going to have lessons for them both.

When it comes to "owning your stuff," a general rule is that if you see it in your partner, if it's in your face, you have something to learn.

Finances are another good example. One of you is a spendthrift, the other tight-fisted. But you both have issues with money and much to teach one another, you see?

Pairings are so often a manifestation of opposite tendencies come together. And this is no accident. For each one can help the other find the middle way.

Call this compromise, if you will. But do not think compromise in this sense is a "selling out" of any kind—which is often what your ego is going to tell you. Or anyone who has an investment in your staying the same.

Compromise of this sort is about finding balance in terms of your own polarity through one who has the opposite charge on a given issue. It's not about one or the other giving in, but rather both people growing towards a center. And from that balanced centerpoint, difficulties dissolve, struggles subside and a new lesson will arise.

Divorcing yourself from a problem or a person doesn't diminish it at all, however. You may feel that is the only option you have in particularly desperate circumstances, but life will find a way to serve up that lesson again and again—in a new form, perhaps, but the same lesson nevertheless.

Resolving issues, coming to terms, is not nearly as difficult as you think it has to be. Therapy or counseling of some kind may be helpful. Guidance of all kinds exists. But the key is acknowledging the mystery in one another and in your relationship. Knowing a higher purpose is at work (and not knowing how it works or where it will take you) is all you really need for things to shift.

It is so simple. And yet it is the hardest thing for people to do. Everyone wants what they want when they want it, and they're so busy worrying they won't get it, they cannot seem to get out of their own way.

Want what you want. And let it go. Be open to what life can show you through another and you may find yourself on the receiving end of more than you ever imagined. More happiness, more joy, *more of what your soul longs for* than you ever knew.

This is true abundance—it's not about material wealth at all. Not that there's anything wrong with material things per se, they just can never satisfy the needs of the soul. (And it may take the experience of extremes in the material world for one to really know that.)

Balance. Compromise. Belief in some power outside yourselves working towards good. These are the things that enable love to endure, that help two people find their way together. No material thing can do that.

So, when you would give a gift of love, let it be something of yourself given with an open heart and not merely that which can be wrapped up and tied with a bow. If you know what your partner desires in their innermost being, let this be what you offer.

In giving it, you will find yourself receiving something in return that's exactly what your soul longs for, though you know it not. In the very moment of giving you shall receive—because, in the moment of giving, a part of you opens to receive gifts beyond measure. Being willing to give and open to receiving go hand in hand. Think about that next time you would demand something from your partner.

Four

Become Aware of Your Unconscious Intentions

SO OFTEN WHEN two people marry, one or the other or both are looking to be taken care of, whether they're consciously aware of it or not. And yet they really are meant to bring forth their souls through this union. So in a sense, each partner is required to have the qualities of a parent, not a child. To care for another and themselves in the process.

Marriage and the word *matrimony* have their roots in, can be traced back to, the word for mother. How appropriate for a process that gives birth to the soul, that brings forth the divine in each of us, so that it can be consciously integrated into our everyday lives.

This is what marriage is truly intended to be. This is the challenge couples face. And if you find yourself married and struggling *without* an awareness that this is the true purpose of what you have engaged in, you are going to be very unhappy.

On the other hand, if you see this as the highest purpose the two of you can have, if you are conscious that your agreement with one another is to do no less than give birth to your souls so that they may become fully present in the world, then every other choice you make, every interaction between you is going to be different—profoundly different—than it otherwise would be.

It is the case that there are many who are only dimly aware that there's a higher calling here than the world recognizes. It is also true that many of these same people discover this almost by accident—because it is essential that they do so. It becomes apparent that only this larger purpose, only a higher power at work can save them from themselves, from the conflicts and crises they create as each seeks to be taken care of by the other, to have the needs of the personality met without regard for what one is there to give. Couples go to great lengths to indulge one another's fantasies in this regard. (The language of lovers can be quite revealing.) Yet it is fundamentally disempowering to be indulged in illusion.

Rather, they should examine their willingness to take on the responsibility of a parent to, of mother to, of giving birth to, the soul. How different their behavior will become if this is what they take on.

Instead of seeking to be taken care of by another, one seeks to take care; instead of a preoccupation with one's own wants and needs, the wants and needs of the partner become primary. One gives oneself over to what is best for the relationship, one gives oneself to its highest expression of truth and love. Not in the way that so many of you fear, as in the obliteration of the self—but in a way that nurtures the true self, in a way that allows you to see that what serves the relationship, what serves the marriage, also serves your own highest good.

Assume the qualities of the mother, not the child. Take on the role of a nurturer, whether you are a husband or a wife, and you shall find yourself nurtured (though not necessarily indulged) in ways that really matter. You will find your marriage takes on new meaning and renews itself in every way. You will find what so many are seeking, but few know how to find, and that is the depth of fulfillment that comes from knowing why you are here.

For though you may have other callings in life, other gifts to give the world, if you are married, you have chosen to share the task of bringing your two souls more completely into consciousness, into the world. Without an awareness of this sacred purpose, marriages are, indeed, difficult and do not endure.

Marriage is not something to play at, nor is it a game of "change partners." It is nothing less than two people helping one another find their way home. To soul. To God.

Do not berate yourselves if this has not been your awareness or intention. But ask yourselves if it is something you are willing to do.

If not, your struggles shall remain the same. For unless you infuse your marriage with this highest of intentions, you do not find the grace that allows you to transcend your own egos, your own small selves.

It is really these small selves that are creating the drama, the difficulty, the pain. It is like *The War of the Roses*, with little to be gained.

Once you have the conscious intention of soul growth, however, there is no war to be won. There is no fear of losing yourself, for your true self is free to emerge.

With the conscious intention of soul growth, love does not diminish, passion does not fade, people do not grow apart but, instead, find that each is a kind of disciple of the other. And, in this way, does each make the other whole, by contributing to their growth, nurturing their soul, showing them a vision of themselves—a soul vision—that alone they cannot see.

It is a holy thing, marriage. This is what you must remember. It is to be celebrated. It is to be honored. And yes, most of all it needs to be recognized for all that it is in your half-asleep world.

Consider this your wakeup call, if you like.

Five

Be Willing to Look at What Your Relationship Reveals about You

AS LONG AS couples are preoccupied with meeting the needs of the personality and not the soul, they are in a constant struggle to attain what in no way can satisfy them at a deep level. Being dissatisfied, they often sabotage their partnerships—consciously and unconsciously. And, once sabotaged, the relationship is reduced to a sorting out of who gets what in their parting.

How sad that what could save them is something they cannot see. For they suffer greatly. And they are not the only ones who suffer when this process of disintegration occurs.

Clearly, it is most difficult when they have children, but even when they do not have children, the collective consciousness, the whole of humanity, is affected. The impact of divorce on other couples trying to find their way cannot be underestimated.

Although many couples are working consciously and working things out and making a difference,the overwhelming attitude in the culture regarding marriage has to do with beating the odds. It is seen as a matter of sheer luck if a marriage survives. Or a matter of being married to the "right" person (which many a divorced person is in search of, by the way), when in fact, the key to marriage that lasts is within you.

As with any journey of the soul, the temptation to make it about external causes and conditions is constant. But, again, as with any journey of the soul, the answers can only be found by looking within.

Even those who have an inkling that this is the case are often quite reluctant to do the work their own souls require of them. Because often what the soul demands is changing one's life in ways that can be quite threatening to the personality.

If you are living in a way that meets all of your material needs, for example, but does not provide one ounce of inspiration for your soul, demands will arise from within you to change that. These same demands will often appear to be coming from your partner when, in fact, he or she is not the source but merely the mirror.

A willingness to see this, to honor the part of yourself that is starved out, can only be good for the relationship. And yet many find it easier to find fault and lay blame than simply look at what another is revealing to them and act on it. This is a scenario that plays itself out over and over again in relationships—until one sees the light, as it were.

In fact, people often experience different partners as mirroring the same things back to them, much to their dismay.

But this is the nature of soul. It has desires that are quite independent from those of the personality. In every experience, in every situation you find yourself in, your soul is giving you an opportunity to see where it would take you. It will show you—in a myriad of different ways, including the partner as mirror—the direction in which you need to move, the way in which you must change your life, for a closer alignment to soul. You may choose a circuitous route, you may make many detours, and resistance may take many forms, but always—always—the soul is showing you what it needs for its own fulfillment.

So when your partner offers up something you'd rather not see in yourself—and your partner can, indeed, be a constant reminder of where your growth is—ask yourself if you would starve your soul. For in this experience, you are entirely capable of—if you are willing to look at what it is you are being shown—fulfilling your own deepest desires.

That is what surprises so many of you. You enter a relationship expecting *another* to fulfill your desires, when in fact their gift will be to show you what your soul's desire is in order that *you* may fulfill it, in order that you may live in a way that furthers who you really are. More than a few of you are disappointed to learn this. Nevertheless, you are all self-actualizing. Another cannot do for you what you must do for yourself.

The gift a partner has for you is that through their love and their ability to see your soul and to mirror your inner being (through no choice of their own but rather through grace), they point the way. They are the guiding star in what would otherwise be a sea of loneliness and confusion.

This is not to say that such partnership is the only

way of finding solace, guidance or companionship, but that loneliness is what makes you so willing to embrace another, to embark on this journey of a lifetime that is marriage.

Look to your partner as one looks to a higher power when seeking solace. Let down your defenses for a moment and consider that this power is working in and through them to show you what, alone, you cannot see.

Be grateful for their willing participation in your life, in your soul journey. Be grateful for what they offer you. And, on seeing what you have to learn about your true nature, bless them. For they, like you, are struggling in the same way. And your willingness to see, your appreciation of their contribution, helps them to move forward, helps them to see, helps them to become aware of what life is asking them to do.

Be conscious that your holding back is reciprocated also. Call this karma, if you will.But as you do to another, so shall it be done unto you. And by yourself alone. This is how things work.

Though many of you know this on some level, it is so often forgotten precisely when it's most important. And that is what keeps people stuck in patterns they can't seem to break out of.

Seek to remain conscious when it is hardest for you to do so and your effort will be rewarded greatly. Everything in the Universe will support you, if only you let it. Intention is the key. The smallest step in this direction of willingness to see and trust in what is being shown to you can shake even the oldest pattern to its foundation.

Conscious intention is always more powerful than unconscious behavior, because that is the direction of the soul, the direction of God, the flow of the entire Universe. And, as they say, it's much easier to ride the horse in the direction it's going.

Make the effort to become conscious. It is the only way. Do not take your partner for granted. Do not think it beyond them to show you yourself in this way. There is more to them than you will ever know, as there is more to you than you are aware of. Your journey together is but one aspect, one dimension, of the mystery. But no less important than any other.

Six

Finding Your Way with Another Requires Going within Yourself

PARTNERSHIPS ARE complex. There are subtleties, nuances and a great many unspoken things "between the lines," one might say. You would do well to remember that a partner can always feel the truth of your exchange. Or the lack of it. Your intentions are felt. And words that contradict them won't count for much.

The irony here is that for all the words that fly between you, most of you don't communicate consciously with each other regarding your intentions for one another or for your marriage.

It is very important to do this, to share your vision of the relationship, to share your innermost desires and your dream for the two of you. In this way, you will maintain the vitality of your marriage. And holding this shared vision will become the focal point for everything else you do, a tool for evaluating the many choices that the two of you will make together.

Imagine how many conflicts and disagreements would be easier to deal with, if not eliminated altogether, if you were to hold them up to a shared vision. Authentic agreement makes for great clarity between the two of you as to how you would live your lives, what to retain and value and nurture in your relationship. And what to discard.

The mind of your personality cannot do this. It has its own agenda. But a vision that comes from your deepest, truest self, from your soul, is a powerful tool for guidance, for evaluating what serves your marriage and what doesn't.

Often, you'll find the concerns of the personality seem irrelevant in this light, along with the unconscious behavior and the cultural "shoulds" you have brought to the table. In fact, the more you refine this vision, this way of being, the more you'll find there are few if any rules to be applied.

Each couple's particular circumstances, along with each couple's particular and unique vision, is going to count for more than anything other people say is good or not good for a marriage.

This kind of reassessment is long overdue for most of you. And, indeed, while there are those who are working quite consciously to help couples through their difficulties, there is also a lot in mass culture about how to have a successful marriage that is pure bunk. It has no value to anyone but people selling magazines.

To develop a shared vision with your partner, however, takes time. First you must be very clear what your own vision is, what your soul's point of view is and how it is distinct from your ego's. This is no small thing.

Assuming you begin to understand that distinction, a period of reflection is in order. For only when you're satisfied that your vision is one of clarity can you begin to share it and shape it and arrive at a vision that is large enough for the two of you.

Both partners have much to offer here, much to contribute to one another. But the sad truth is that one or the other of you may feel inadequate and have little awareness of your gifts or your true capacity for love, until you engage in this soul-searching process. Indeed, both of you may feel this way.

This soul-searching process entails far more than quiet time or relaxation. It requires a sincere heart and an ability to open yourself to the great mystery of who you really are and why you have chosen to be here, what it is you would do with your life.

These are the questions all people must answer for themselves. Dogma does not suffice. Settling for another's answer will not do. There is no substitute for what is in you, what is in your own heart, particularly when you would take on the task of sharing your soul with another in this lifetime. (This is why so many people find their religious beliefs fail them when they are in crisis or when their relationship is being tested. They have adopted something that is not their own.)

Discovering the truth in your own heart, in your own soul, demands that you find a way to get in touch with that part of yourself. There are many tools that enable one to do this, and when they are sought sincerely, they will be revealed to you. But none is simpler or more powerful than prayer.

Now, for all too many of you, prayer has become something of an anachronism. You'd rather meditate or take workshops that purport to have all the answers and the power to transform your lives. But, indeed, prayer is as powerful as it ever was. And it is as relevant to the sophisticated modern with no sense of connection to the Divine as it is to those humble servants of God who lived in simpler times. (Indeed, many such souls exist today as well. They live quietly, doing their soul work far from television cameras and news commentators. They haven't turned their backs on the world either, but have chosen a life with fewer distractions from their spiritual path.)

Prayer is acknowledgment that invites divine assistance. Prayer transcends your circumstances whatever they might be. Anyone can experience the power of prayer. Father-Mother God, the great spirit, the Universe, is totally ready to support you in every way if only you let it.

Pray to be open. Pray to discover your purpose, your gift, your reason for living. Pray that you may be guided to a knowledge of what is in your own soul, what is appropriate for your deepest inner being, your essential self—the one that transcends the body you now find yourself in, the life you are now living, the mind of the particular personality you have created for this particular adventure.

Pray for guidance, and all manner of things will begin to show yourself to you. Your partner, most especially. And thus do you begin to see the divine in one another, thus do you begin to transform your relationship in earnest, to transcend your small selves.

Do this and you will come to know a satisfaction in your lives that nothing outside you can offer. Do this and you will experience a vital force that pours forth in abundance if only you allow it.

Let it sustain you. Let it guide you. Let it take you into the mystery of yourself and of another; into the mystery of All That Is. For such is your reason for being here—to awaken to the Divine. To draw it into your life and into the world. To contribute your own unique expression and vision and passion to that which is God.

This is a holy thing. This is something no one does in isolation. And, yes, it is what lies at the center of the sacred bond of marriage. Whatever else two people may share, they are doing the work of bringing their souls more completely into the world.

If you think otherwise, you are kidding yourselves. If you think otherwise, do not embark on this path.

If marriage *is* your choice, however, go to the center. Embrace the truth of your soul. Your partner will follow. For, in being in your truth, you shall eliminate the need for any resistance they might have with you.

Once in the center, you can see each other as you really are. You will find, again, that being you first beheld in love, that soul you would share yourself with, that soul with whom you are one.

Go to the center. Begin the soul sharing. All that is irrelevant will fall away. And all that was wounded will be healed.

Seven

Marriage Is a Journey into the Mystery of Your Soul

To participate in the process of sharing souls, one must be willing to deal with the resistance that arises within the personality. It is precisely this resistance which causes you conflict and pain in your relationships. These things are much easier to deal with, however, once you recognize the three very distinct phases of relationship.

The first phase is commonly called bliss. That's because it's a euphoric state, as most relationships arise within a condition of grace. And, indeed, there is much joy in this. There is an opening of the heart that allows the two of you to come together with your defenses down. You are quite open to each other, in spite of yourselves, you might say. And, in this open heart space, you have a deep sense of soul—of your own soul and that of your partner. (Though many of you don't consciously recognize it as such.)

It is this openness, this suspension of the ego, which allows you to see in each other the very qualities you've thought lacking in yourself, the very qualities that will complete you and make you whole. (In fact, you do possess these qualities within yourself, but they are unexpressed or less developed than other qualities that are serving the soul's primary purpose in this lifetime.)

This mutual attraction of souls, in a sense, overrides all the doubts and fears of the small self. It allows you to see another as perhaps no one else sees them. And a part of you recognizes in them the promise of your own completion.

This phenomenon you call "falling in love" is the only aspect of relationship that is acknowledged and celebrated in your world. However, it is not so much falling as joining. The ego falls away, your defenses dissolve and a bond between souls is realized for purposes that few of you ever imagine.

It is this bond that you are acknowledging when you choose to participate in the marriage rituals of any culture. But the ritual is just that—acknowledgment of what has already happened. The ritual itself has no power to create such a union.

There are those of you who have an authentic bond but do not feel a need to ritualize it in any public way. Your union is no less real, no less sacred. As long as it is completely acknowledged and honored by the two of you.

It is only when people are forced into marriages that are not of their own choosing that no sacred union, as such, exists. And so, to assume the enlivening process of soul sharing can occur in such circumstances is a mistake. (Such arrangements may serve other purposes in one's life, but they are not what we are discussing here.)

The bonding phase of relationship is a blissful, inspired and gentle one. It is also characterized by a quality of recognition—one knows the other though they know not how. Yet this phase is only one aspect of relationship.

In the second phase, or what could be called the identity phase, a resurgence of ego comes into play. At this time, your need for autonomy reasserts itself. This is a natural part of the relationship process. However, difficulty arises when couples in this phase compare their situation to the first, more blissful, state and feel a loss.

Yet this second phase is as essential as the first. It is only by preserving your individuality within the context of your union that you can come to know the desires of your own soul.

In this phase, much of what you have assumed yourself to be is challenged. And a kind of burnishing takes place. The qualities which are most in the way of your growth are, in a sense, dissolved, worn away, through daily interaction—and often conflict—with your partner. Each of you is constantly forced to choose that which is more important—the quality or trait in question, or the life of the relationship.

This does not mean your personality is obliterated or that either partner should submit to the other's wish for them to change (or remain unchanged from the initial stage of bliss). Rather, those things that limit you, that block the full expression of your soul, are brought forth and reflected back to you by the partner so you may see yourself in a way that you haven't before.

Upon seeing anything that doesn't really serve you or the relationship, you may choose to surrender it. But understand you are not giving anything up for your partner, but for yourself. Any sacrifice you make is for the redemption of your own soul.

This process challenges both partners equally. It favors neither of you, furthers both of you, in that you are being distilled, refined and reshaped in terms of what serves the relationship, what serves the soul. They are one in the same in this case.

On the surface, this may look like a real mess. Frequently people find it easier to find fault with their partner than to face what is in themselves that needs reevaluation. And so conflict is common. Indeed, it is the defining characteristic of this second phase of relationship.

But make no mistake—something quite powerful is going on. Something you could never do alone, something that is forcing each of you to be true to yourselves in a way you could never have anticipated. You are shedding every illusion that stands in the way of true self.

Still, love endures—that's the miracle. Still, the bond is strong—stronger than before. For soul growth nurtures it in a way no illusion can. And two people who are nurturing each other's souls in this way are two who will endure. Despite what the culture says, despite their imperfections, even despite the pain they cause one another, equally, in this most difficult contest of wills. (Again, not the will of one partner over another; rather, the struggle is between the will of the personality and the more authentic requirements of the soul.)

This is the crucible of marriage. This is "the work for which all other work is merely preparation" (Rilke). It is the forging of a new identity that serves the soul through the forging of a new identity that serves the relationship. One cannot distinguish between the two—they are one and the same.

This is what makes marriage sacred. The soul work it enables is profound. It is truly an expression of divine purpose. And coming into an awareness of this is vital if two people are to forgive all manner of suffering they will experience in this crucial Phase Two.

The willingness to forgive, the knowledge of a higher purpose in your relationship and the choice to surrender to it (not to the partner, but to the highest self), redeems the mess you make of your marriage and both of you in it.

Redemption of the spirit, becoming your soul, finding your way home to God is difficult work— not because it has to be, but because human beings make it so. The ego puts up quite a fight. And yet it is only through enduring love for another that one is willing to give up that which they never really were.

Next time you ponder what someone sees in another, think on this. For so it is with all of you. You've chosen endless illusions and disguises. And yet your partner sees your soul, your partner mirrors every part of you, enabling you to choose who it is you would become. This gift of love is nothing less than holy.

> *When people get married because they think it's a long-time love affair, they'll be divorced very soon, because all love affairs end in disappointment. But marriage is recognition of a spiritual identity. . . . Marriage means the two are one. . . . If you are acquiescing constantly to it instead of individual whim, you come to realize this is true—the two really are one.*
>
> Joseph Campbell*

There is a third phase of marriage as well. One that is not experienced but by a few of you, yet one that holds all promise and hope and fulfillment for everyone on this path. And that is a third phase in which the true nature of your soul finds expression and the true purpose for which any two of you have come together in this lifetime may emerge.

This last phase in the circle of the marriage relationship is a kind of return in order to experience in much fuller awareness and deep joy that which grace granted a glimpse of in your initial coming together. And that is your soul's most loving, joyful nature, which would express in its own unique way a particular gift to your fellow human beings.

There will be much said with regard to the matter of the sacred purpose, the soul dream to make real in subsequent texts and teachings; however, it is most

* *The Power of Myth.* (N. Y.: Doubleday, 1988) p. 6.

helpful to know that this, too, is where marriage, the sacred union, ultimately leads.

For, as in all matters of the soul, it is the life purpose, the sacred purpose, which seeks to emerge. And, as marriage is intended to reveal and to make conscious the soul awareness, it is a natural outcome, an intentional byproduct, if you will, a most fulfilling and consequential result of your partnering for both of you.

This is to say that when conflict gives way to acceptance and soul growth is nurtured, there is a flowering that takes the form of a great gift to the world. A unique gift that it is your desire and, indeed, your delight to bring forth, to make real. And it is the case, also, that partners not only serve to facilitate this for one another; their gifts are mutually reinforcing, exquisitely compatible, beautifully and jointly experienced, enhanced and appreciated and, yes, furthered when they are shared—not just exclusively within the partnership, but with everyone your lives touch.

In other words, you help one another to be and become all that it is your dream to be and do in the world in this life. Whether it is a seemingly small contribution to the lives of those you are closest to or a great gift for all humanity.

It is the sacred journey you make together that allows the best that is in you, the highest good, to be recognized, to be brought forth, to be shared, to be given away in order that you may be fulfilled deep in your soul for this expression of your true self that is so arduously sought, hard won and, in truth, the only thing that can really fulfill the deep longing you have felt all your life.

It is a most beautiful thing, this Self-realization that is so powerfully enabled by another and by your willingness to become who you really are out of your true and enduring love for them.

Indeed, you could not keep such a phenomenon as this to yourselves even if you wanted to. For it is evident to any who can really see you, any who can receive this gift of your Self and your having become love. Yes, love personified, the embodiment of love, the union of love and light, of spirit and matter, man and woman, mortal and divine child of the Universe.

It is no less than this profound completion, this joining of heaven and earth, that marriage may, indeed, take you to. And if you take only the smallest step in this direction, if you even begin to feel the power of this completion phase, it will be as the most incredible experience you have ever known. As we have said, it is a holy thing, marriage. And, as such, it carries within it the keys to the kingdom, as it were.

Think on this when you would walk away or cry out in anger and, indeed, you will find a great desire within you to carry on.

Eight

Surrendering to Your Relationship Is Surrendering to Your Soul

This is love: to fly toward a secret sky,
to cause a hundred veils to fall each moment.
First to let go of life.
Finally, to take a step without feet.

Rumi*

THE LONGING IN the heart to draw nearer to God is the universal human condition, though it is often disguised as longing for another mortal human being.

Realize it is the divine soul in the beloved that you are drawn to. That you and your partner are both a manifestation of God in this world. And that the ultimate task the two of you share is to become fully conscious of this and live from this awareness as much as it is humanly possible.

All else is illusion. All else is for the purpose of learning and leading you to this truth. All else is the drama you create for your own benefit—though you may not know it at the time. That is because much of what you create is the result of unconscious intention.

Becoming conscious is the goal. And your partner will do much to make you aware of, conscious of, what's operating in you at an unconscious level. The fact that you love them, and they you, is what makes

* *The Ruins of the Heart,* Selected Lyric Poetry of Jelàuddin Rumi, translated by Edmund Helminski (Aptos, Calif.: Threshold Books, 1981). Used by permission.

this exchange possible. For being confronted with your own shadow is a very threatening thing for most people. It gives rise to fears of every kind. And it is only when there is a context of love and support—a sense of deep, authentic sharing—that one is able to embrace the lessons life would offer them.

This condition of trust is fundamental in a marriage in order to realize its sacred dimension. And yet trust is precisely what is so often damaged in the conflicts that arise between two who would make a life together.

It is not easy for one who feels threatened to stand back and consider that the most difficult truths their partner is showing them, revealing to them in myriad ways continually, are truly those things that the soul would heal in order to make them whole. It is difficult to accept that, as Joseph Campbell put it, "Where your pain is, there is your life also." And yet this is the real drama of marriage.

When you are tempted to dismiss your issues or problems as trite, realize they are far from this. Rather, the underlying issue is showing you a side of yourself that must be faced, must be reckoned with, for your own good, for your own growth.

Learn to distinguish this underlying truth from the many forms it may take in your day-to-day exchange. Learn to help each other do this with gentleness and compassion. For it is often true that your partner is struggling with the same lesson, but approaching it from an opposite perspective.

No wonder, then, that at times you'll feel this opposition as a challenge to everything you hold yourself to be. This is precisely when it is most difficult—and most critical—that you take a deep breath and say to yourself: There is something for me to learn from this experience. Something that will ultimately benefit me if I can take it in, if I can allow for the possibility that what is happening is revealing to me exactly what I need to know at this time for my deepest purpose of growth and fullest expression of joy. It is more important than any defense I might utter. It is showing me my path to God.

In taking just that moment to break the reactive pattern of the personality, a world of possibility opens up. The support of the entire Universe flows in to enable the learning in light and love. It heals. It lifts. It reinforces your sense of connection to the Divine in order that you may rise to the next lesson more easily.

With each moment of opening, that part of you that desires to move forward will grow stronger. With each moment of opening to your own soul, the gap between who you are and who you think you are diminishes.

More and more of you will find yourselves truly appreciating what is coming to you in the form of your partner. That person whom you've granted the power to make you crazy like no other (with the possible exception of your parents) shall be the very one who reveals the path to redeeming your spirit, knowing your soul and living more fully in the awareness that you and God are one.

It is as simple as a moment's allowing for the possibility. There need be no more than that for partners to turn their pain, their problems, to good.

And with each moment of opening, the love is stronger. With each moment of opening, the passion of the soul returns. With each moment of opening to the possibility that your partner is God in disguise and is offering you something of great value, your sense of being deeply, deeply loved will become more real to you.

For it is only your sense of separation and the resistance of the personality that keep you from knowing this, from feeling it in every aspect of your being, at all times.

Your partner, then, is your constant reminder that this other you is your true nature, your true self. If only you were open to it. And it is somewhat natural for human beings to resent a constant reminder. Nevertheless, it is required. Be thankful for it and come to appreciate your partner as one who enables your soul work with love—though it may look like something else entirely at any given moment.

Allow yourself to see them as a teacher of life lessons designed specifically for you. Allow. Allow. Allow. It is the key to finding your way through the darkness of conflict and pain. And it is not so difficult afterall. As human beings are so fond of saying, even a child can do it.

Nine

Transcend Your Cultural Conditioning

THE COMING INTO awareness that one experiences in this crucible of marriage is, perhaps, the soul's greatest work in the world today. Secular life has replaced many of the traditions of the past which offered a framework for understanding mystical experience and the soul journey all must undertake. But today, outside of those individuals who commit themselves to a solitary spiritual path, most people are encountering their own souls through the process of relationship.

Because the culture offers little in the way of understanding the sacred process that is at work here, it is important for all of you to reexamine the cultural beliefs that you have internalized which are consciously and unconsciously shaping your behavior.

A great deal of what is at work in you is false. Notions of what romantic love is and should be that have achieved widespread popularity are quite far from what most of you really experience in the ongoing relationships you find yourselves in. And, by clinging to these unrealistic notions, these false beliefs, and trying to live up to them, you actually make your relationships more difficult, more painful. For it is the case that no real relationship can live up to such expectations. Nor should it.

At one time, romantic love was held in much higher esteem. And there was a certain amount of truth contained in the archetypal images that pervaded the stories, the legends that people lived by or attempted to live by. Joseph Campbell has had much to say about this, much to offer in the way of interpretation of the symbolic elements of these mythological templates for understanding the soul process that is at work.

But in today's world, there is a preoccupation with the sensual and the sexual which, sadly, overshadows the real purpose, the divine purpose, which is at the heart of the sacred union.

This is not to say that the sensual and sexual aspects of relationship are insignificant, but rather they are no end in themselves. If one seeks merely to have one's sexual appetites satisfied, one's sexual needs fulfilled, there are easier ways to do this than to engage in a long-term commitment to another's happiness and well being in all aspects of life—in sickness and in health, and so on. Yet there are many of you who measure the success or failure of your marriage in precisely these terms.

There are also many of you who measure your relationships in material terms. As well, there are those of you who seek to be taken care of, who make trade-offs and confine yourselves to playing roles that severely limit your soul's expression, not to mention growth.

There are many justifications for this, the most common being the desire to create a stable environment in which to raise children. And yet what an unconscious relationship tells children is that it is all right to suffocate the soul, to live without authenticity and inspiration, to act the part rather than open yourself to living in a way that has deep meaning. This causes much pain and loss for all concerned. Wounding of the sort that imprints a lifetime is the legacy these children inherit.

Fortunately, there is little in the way of reinforcement for these patterns in today's culture. However, they are the cultural ideals that most influenced most of your parents. And, as such, they are still present in many of you today.

These are the things—and there are many more—which operate at some level in your being, which you bring to your relationship whether you're aware of it or not. Both of you must be willing to examine these hidden influences and hold them up to what is in your own hearts, to choose consciously what you would live by in order to free your own souls.

This needn't be a difficult or painful process. But it must be done. It is otherwise the case that these beliefs are driving your behavior at some level whether you want them to or not.

Still, at some point, your soul will assert itself, whether you have embraced it willingly or not. If you "prepare the way," as it's said, this can be a most welcome phenomenon. If not, it can be the undoing, the unraveling, of everything you think yourself to be, everything you think your life to be.

This kind of crisis, while not uncommon, is not necessary either. But it seems to be what it takes for some of you to become aware of who you really are.

The tragedy here is that these are often the same people who've brought children into the world quite unaware of their obligations and responsibilities in doing so. For there are agreements between souls. And an agreement to bring a child into this world is among the most sacred. Failing awareness, one cannot provide all that is required for the development of a child's sense of self in the world.

So it is that this subject of marriage is truly at the heart of things. For it is shaping the world in the most fundamental ways, two at a time, in every family all around the planet. To realize its true purpose—which is to enliven your soul—is to allow the world to become what it was always intended to be: an expression of the best that is in you, an expression of the divine in us all.

Ten

Honor Love—It Is the Highest Calling

WHEN TWO PEOPLE become aware of the true purpose of marriage and open themselves to soul process, the entire Universe supports them. Things that wouldn't have seemed possible come to pass. Issues that they struggled with seem not nearly as important as they once were. And the element of grace is present in their relationship once more. A grace that allows them to see from a new perspective and to move forward where there were blocks and seeming dead ends before.

It takes their relationship to a new level where the soul work itself inspires them to a different, and sometimes very unconventional, way of living their daily lives. It frees them from previous conditions and constraints and breathes new life into their daily existence. It also impacts those around them—children, especially—in a way that inspires divine purpose through simple, joyous affection and understanding.

The fight goes out of them, you might say. The fight to preserve the ego, the fight to control a process that is beyond anyone's control, the fight to win, to come out on top, to be right—in order to deceive themselves, in order to avoid discovering the mystery of their deepest selves.

There is a freedom of great magnitude. It is what is suggested in the notion, in story and song, of being tied to someone or something else in order to be free. By joining with your partner in a renewed effort to have your marriage work for your highest purpose, you begin anew.

This is not to say that you have a blank slate, but that direction and guidance will emerge through the opening of your hearts and minds that enlivens and inspires every aspect of your lives. This may be a subtle phenomenon or it may be a resounding one, depending on the individuals involved. But it will change your lives nevertheless.

For alignment with the soul is the most powerful force in your world. It is what you come here to discover and to live by. And, though it may take lifetimes, not to mention the assistance of many such life partners as you find yourself with now, it is the only thing that can fulfill you, redeem you and give your life meaning.

It is the work all must do. It is finding God within you. It is the natural outcome of authentic love between two mortal human beings. And it transcends life on earth. For you transcend life on earth. Not the small you, but the soul self that is never separate from God, the Divine, the All in All, but is merely forgotten for a time in order to be found again.

This is what is to be celebrated, honored and respected in committing yourself to marriage. And in witnessing the same. It is no mere social event, but an acknowledgment of the highest calling in one of its infinite forms and flowerings. The vows are sacred. The process is sacred. The soul, your true essence, is sacred. And marriage, as a bond between souls, can never be taken lightly nor dissolved.

The world has forgotten this. But it is time to remember, time to be conscious, time to take up the work for which "all other work is merely preparation" (Rilke). Time to save your own souls hand in hand with another. There is no greater purpose, no greater joy.

> *With the drawing of this Love and the voice of this Calling,*
> *We shall not cease from exploration*
> *And the end of all our exploring*
> *Will be to arrive where we started*
> *And know the place for the first time . . .*
>
> T. S. Eliot

Eleven
The Illusion of Divorce

THE THING ABOUT marriage that many of you forget is that it is chosen. There is a point in a marriage when difficulties arise, when passion seems to fade, that you forget it was your choice to enter into this holiest of contracts.

When you are frustrated and looking for a way out, it's easy to delude yourself into thinking you aren't responsible for your state. Or that it's not binding. That you can walk away without consequence.

At such moments, you are in the throes of an ego that is defending itself with the grandest of excuses for dissolution of a marriage—"I made a mistake. Better to end this before things get any worse."

Now there is a certain humility in this. One is admitting responsibility of a kind. And so you are tempted to believe it is, indeed, what you should do. Yet nothing could be further from the truth.

The truth is that unless there are life-threatening circumstances, you do not serve your soul needs in walking away. No ruse on the part of your ego, which longs to survive at any cost, can change this.

Do what you will, choose what you will. But do not make the mistake of thinking for one moment that walking away will take you in the direction of soul. Walking away will take you in the direction of ego (of small self, of limitation). And after a time, it will prop itself up and resume control of your life. You may learn much from this experience. Many people do. But, eventually, you will again find yourself at a point where the same issues must be confronted, where the problems you walked away from will again be staring you in the face, where the lesson of your soul will again come forth to be chosen or not chosen according to your willingness to learn at any given moment.

You can learn easily or joyfully, or you can create much pain before choosing the lesson. And while there is, indeed, wisdom in every choice—something to be learned, in other words—there is also something to be said for—*much* to be said for—accepting any lesson that flows from such a fundamental and life-altering choice as marriage.

Marriage is not a game. It is not something you can really change your mind about and walk away from because the challenges are too difficult—for you have made it so.

Each time you defer a lesson, the circumstances in which it comes back to you will be more challenging than it was before. Because your resistance has grown, it has been fueled by seemingly authentic decisions on your part that, in reality, were about preserving your ego.

This may sound to you like a harsh indictment. And, in a sense, it is. Not because we would interfere with anyone's right to choose or their right to take on a lesson in their own time, but because the pain that is caused by deluding yourselves in this way is, by far, the biggest reason so many of you suffer from broken marriages today.

When you choose marriage only to walk away when you are on the brink of coming to terms with a soul lesson that has been deferred many times over already, you do such damage and cause such pain to yourselves and your partners that most of you are no longer capable of any more learning on this front for the remainder of this lifetime.

You may find some brief happiness with another. You may find you are "better off alone," to quote more than a few of you, but this is not the truth.

The truth is that you have missed an opportunity to resolve an issue that has been with you in many life times, that you have removed yourself from a situation that you set up precisely in order to learn that lesson, that you have squandered all manner of blessings that could only come to you in the very place you opt out of, the very situation that you created and, more, that you required to learn.

That is why we are so very adamant on this point. For how many of you would find it easy to walk away knowing this? How many of you would carry to your grave the lesson unlearned, yet again?

Life is a precious gift. It is a gift for learning, for bringing the soul into full awareness. It is worth more than you know (even though you fear death so). The sacred marriage is, likewise, an opportunity for bringing the soul into awareness.

To think for one moment that a choice to break the sacred bond of marriage is anything but cowardice in so many disguises is to deny everything you knew to be true in your heart when you entered into this covenant.

Yet in your world people think nothing of doing just that. There is no shame in it, no remorse. And yet there will forever be a question that plagues you— Did I give up just as giving in, surrendering my last weapon, would have saved me? Just as I was about to transform my life? Just as I was about to discover who it is that I would become if I were truly free?

The illusions of freedom can look so much more appealing than the real thing. And there is much in the culture to reinforce such illusions. Much in your unconsciousness or being less than awake that allows one to succumb.

But marriage as a sacred bond is not something you can ever walk away from—though it may appear that indeed you have, that you are quite finished with it.

Your lesson will not only come around again, you will remain tied to the one you chose, though you may never see him or her again. There will be an incompleteness that stays with you for the rest of your days, no matter what else you might do. For you will have turned your back on the opportunity to process consciously together all that will continue to pass between you by virtue of the soul bond the two of you created.

Giving up, walking away, will always be a choice you have. But be aware that it is not the harmless choice you like to think it is. Be aware that when a marriage is an authentic one, it is truly a bond that can't be broken in this lifetime. Be aware that many of you who are together have been together before, and if your relationship is particularly challenging, it is quite possible that you are completing the lessons you walked away from in the past. Would you make them any more difficult?

Be aware that what may look to you like the easy way out, or a valid one, at least, is likely to be profoundly painful in the long run.

We would make this difficult truth known in order that you may choose to spare yourself this particular kind of pain and suffering. For it is not necessary, it is not required in order to learn. It is merely the case that pain is what prompts you to learn, what brings you to a state of humility and grace and surrender that allows your divine soul to flow in.

How you learn is up to you. Do not forget this truth. It can serve you well.

Twelve
Your Marriage Has an Impact Far Beyond the Two of You

MARRIAGE, AS it's understood in modern society, is set up to fail. It is only by recognizing and honoring the spiritual dimension that one has any hope of creating a relationship that endures. And yet this is precisely what isn't recognized today—the spiritual dimension.

Although remnants of an earlier understanding are still contained in the rituals of the marriage ceremony, for most people the rituals are hollow, if not irrelevant to their personal beliefs. Beliefs that are only half-conscious, beliefs that are grounded in cultural misconceptions and illusions.

To reclaim the power, the force, of a ritual that is truly meant to acknowledge a bond between souls, one has to create their own rituals today. And many have attempted to do this. But it is not enough to put together your own words for a ceremony you feel has grown hollow if you do not understand what it is you speak of, what kind of journey it is that you are embarking on with another.

To understand, to truly comprehend what is going on, one must be familiar with the nature of soul and the nature of the soul journey. And that is outside the parameters of what modern culture acknowledges, supports and cultivates. This means doing your homework, if you will.

It means devoting as much of yourself to understanding your true nature as you devote to your job, your family and friends, or any other aspect of your life. Yet so many of you are unwilling to do this. You want the instant solution, the easy way to enlightenment, a Band-Aid for a problem that affects your entire being.

There are no simple solutions. There is no path that is right for everyone. There is no getting around the fact that you must come to know what is in your own soul in order to share it with another. In fact, it is only in becoming intimate with yourself in this way that you are truly able to recognize the soul of another.

Until then, you may often respond to another person in ways you hope are the fulfillment of your deepest longing. But, until you take responsibility for acknowledging what is in you that desires complete and open expression, you cannot create the kind of intimacy with another that furthers the development of soul.

Of course, there are times when the cart may seem to come before the horse, as it's said. When the most basic understanding of Self, the faintest inklings of soul, give rise to situations that greatly accelerate this process, and it is the discovery of soul that is shared by two. Such relationships are not unusual and often endure, but they are not what could be called mature, in that there is a certain amount of floundering that limits the depth and scope of the relationship.

Mature, committed relationships, on the other hand, between two who have made their marriage the priority in their lives, who understand that everything necessarily goes back to the two of them as one— these are the ones who lift the rest into fullness and infinite possibility. They are the carriers of the form, the holders of the energy and the power that transforms marriage and soul partnership for all others, for everyone engaged in this particular process of becoming more whole, more authentic, more of who they are in their deepest being.

For them, too, there is much value in this teaching. It is not only meant as a corrective for limited understanding or help for those couples who have lost their way and would find it back again. It is also meant as a powerful reinforcement, an infusion of energy for those who would preserve the sacredness of this institution of marriage, who would seek to become examples and teachers and facilitators for anyone who desires to understand what is really going on here.

It is intended to bring about a remembering and a rediscovery of what has been lost and a renewal of spirit that heals the broken bonds and broken dreams of an entire culture—a mass culture—that has no conception of what it is to see God in yourself or in another.

There are exceptions, to be sure. But the predominant influence in your world is not that of the highest levels of understanding and enlightenment, but that of the lowest. That is what mass culture is. And that is why so little of it is satisfying, so little of it endures, so little of it amounts to anything in the long run.

It is time to recognize this. It is time to change this. And there is no more powerful force for change than an enlightened view of, an expanded awareness and understanding of, other human beings—one at a time.

Begin with your heart's desire. Follow it to your soul's oldest, deepest longing and you will make such a difference in your life and in your world as to inspire the very sun to rise and the birds to sing.

It is time. You who would take another "to have and to hold from this day forward" have much to give the world. Begin it.

Psalm 1

Blessed are the man and the woman
who have grown beyond their greed
and have put an end to their hatred
and no longer nourish illusions.
But they delight in the way things are
and keep their hearts open, day and night.
They are like trees planted near flowing rivers,
which bear fruit when they are ready.
Their leaves will not fall or wither.
*Everything they do will succeed.**

* *"Psalm One,"* translated by Stephen Mitchell, from *The Enligtened Heart,* by Stephen Mitchell, copyright © 1989 by Stephen Mitchell. Reprinted by permission of HarperCollins Publishers, Inc.

Book Two

PREPARING THE WAY

Teachings on Our Sacred Contract with Children

Introduction

The subject of children is one that is dear to the hearts of many. In fact, there are few things about which opinions and beliefs are more strongly held.

And yet it is also the case that there is a kind of crisis in the world today in that many, many children are not receiving even the most basic care they need to survive, to live as healthy, whole people.And there are even more who suffer from a lack of spiritual nourishment despite a certain level of material comfort.

It is for these reasons that we would speak to what it is that children require from everyone. For, indeed, children are everyone's responsibility.

They have gifts to give the world that certainly everyone can benefit from—if the world's children are truly nurtured in ways that not only allow them to live happy, healthy lives, but also to discover their reason for being here and, supported in every way, to bring their gifts forward, to make their unique contributions to the planet and to us all.

Parents also require the support of the larger community, of any society that would fulfill its sacred contract with the next generation. (Sadly, not many are doing that today.)

For even the most devoted parent cannot singlehandedly supply everything that a child requires for the development of a strong sense of self in the world. And failing to develop a strong sense of what they are here to give, children not only become lost souls, as it were, wandering in search of what can only be found within, but all of us lose what they would contribute to our lives, what they have to offer in the way of regeneration and renewal and carrying forward the hopes and dreams and wishes of any who would fulfill their life purpose.

Children contribute enormously to life in ways that are felt and seen but not entirely understood. This lack of clarity, this lack of understanding—and in, some cases, lack of appreciation—has resulted in a world where only in a few small societies are people living with the awareness of what is required and, indeed, fulfilling those requirements.

In places like America and Western Europe, those societies that consider themselves the most civilized, children are not faring so well. They are, in fact, suffering greatly. They are, in fact, experiencing a suffocation of the spirit in the midst of an obsession with the material.

As well, there are children in the world whose suffering is, perhaps, more obvious because it takes physical form in those materially impoverished cultures one gets glimpses of on the evening news. And yet often the love and the spiritual nourishment offered these children is far greater than that given to a child who is more easily plopped down in front of a TV.

For all these reasons and more, we are seeking to clarify the sacred contract that *everyone* has with the children of the world. Indeed, it takes a village—and more—to fulfill this most sacred obligation.

It is not merely parents or professionals entrusted with the care of our children who have a responsibility here; it is everyone who lives and breathes on this planet earth.

This is not widely recognized. And yet it is time to change this. Time to bring forth the best that is within us in order to truly make the world a better place for our children—and for ourselves.

For our legacy is one we ourselves shall inherit. We shall find ourselves returning to this world to participate in all we have created, every last one of us. And, while this may challenge our beliefs—indeed, defy our understanding—it is nevertheless the way things work.

And so, any who have not yet discovered the compassion and love that is in their own hearts may choose a more active level of participation and learning out of self-interest. For indeed, what goes around comes around. And it will be your experience to find yourself on the receiving end of that which you do or do not create in the world.

As it has been said, "Do unto others as you would have others do unto you." This is no mere theory for acting "as if." It is true. For, as Christ taught, "As you do [or do not do] unto the least of these, so you do unto me [and unto yourself]."

It is in everyone's best interest to be aware of what we create for our children. To honor them far more than we do. To nurture them in all the ways that are essential for the fulfillment of each life, for the fulfillment of every soul dream a child brings with them to fulfill. It is nothing less than holy, the creation and re-creation of the world in this way. And it is time to be conscious of all it entails.

That is the purpose of these teachings. That is the purpose of life. To make the soul dream real. And there is no more powerful dream than that which arrives in the souls of our children. We can enable them in every way or we can remain blind to their suffering. But whichever we choose, we shall know too. And we will experience the result at our most powerless and vulnerable. For such is the human experience. Every last one of us comes into this world at the mercy of another. We are all in this together. And it is time to live from this awareness as much as humanly possible.

> *So it is not the will of my Father who is in Heaven that one of these little ones should perish.*
>
> Matthew 18:14

One

Not Everyone Is a Parent, but Everyone Has a Sacred Contract with Children

AS WITH SO many close relationships, those between parents and their children are relationships between souls who have made many journeys together and who have agreements at the soul level to complete those lessons that are incomplete between them.

This process of completion may extend over many life times together. And it is often the case that parents and their children will reverse roles in these many life times. It is also common that they appear within the same family over generations, although this is not always the case. But often it is, indeed, the reason for particular affections between grandparents and grandchildren that cannot be otherwise explained. For in every family there is a repetition to varying degrees between all its members and, at this point in human history, you have all shared a great number of life times together in all your families.

People who say in anger, "I didn't ask to be born" or "I didn't choose my parents" or "I didn't ask for this child" are quite mistaken. They are merely unaware of the choices they have made at the soul level.

Indeed, they may even be unaware that they have a soul, not to mention all the ways the soul is quite distinct from the personality or ego they have created for themselves for this time around.

And that is part of the problem, after all. For there is so much that they will experience together that cannot be explained in terms of the psychology of family systems or even the precious family values of so many of the world's religions.

Perhaps Kahlil Gibran came closest to the truth when he said,

Your children are not your children.
They are the sons and daughters of Life's longing for itself.
They come through you but not from you,
*And though they are with you, yet they belong not to you.**

For in saying, "Your children are not your children," he was challenging all the beliefs and, indeed, behaviors that result when the soul purpose of this relationship goes unrecognized.

When the soul purpose of this relationship goes unrecognized, parents see their children as extensions of themselves and seek to live vicariously through them. When the soul purpose is not recognized, children grow up to disown their families. When the soul purpose is not recognized, it cannot be fulfilled. And when it is unfulfilled, it is an incompletion that stands to be worked out again, to be completed in yet another life or another or another.

* From *The Prophet*, by Kahlil Gibran. Copyright 1923 by Kahlil Gibran and renewed 1951 by Administrators C T A of Kahlil Gibran Estate and Mary G. Gibran. Reprinted by permission of Alfred A. Knopf, a Division of Random House Inc.

The difficulty that goes with all this is far beyond human comprehension. It is, perhaps, enough to say that with each repetition, the lessons are more challenging, the purpose for which two lives have come together is more difficult to achieve. Because, in coming around again, there is much unfinished business to attend to in addition to this question of soul purpose. Think on those relationships with your own parents, for example. They are often painful. There isn't always the sense of love and gratitude between you that enables learning without pain. And what most of you do with this is to promise that you will be different with your own children. But few of you really are.

For it is the case that being a parent challenges what you presume yourself to be. It challenges everything you've been taught about what it is to be a good parent. It requires you to live more authentically and to be willing to engage with that unique and powerful soul you have brought into the world in a way that is totally earnest, totally honest, totally sincere, totally flexible, totally present and aware that being authentic in every way is nothing less than your sacred obligation, at least until a child comes of age.

But most do not even attempt to live this way. Most do not do the soul work that enables them to discover what it is to be authentic. And it is not generally acknowledged as a requirement for bringing children into the world. *But it should be.*

For failing in this awareness, all manner of suffering is inflicted on one another quite unconsciously. And no small amount of life energy is drawn away from the soul purpose to repair the damage—much of which is incomplete even at death.

Even those who have every best intention to do the right thing are often operating unconsciously or looking to some outside authority to resolve a question that can only be resolved by full authentic conscious engagement with this being you have brought to life in a state of dependence on you for everything but the autonomy of later years.

Parenting is holy. It is God-making. It is the most sacred contract between any two people on the planet. And it is time for everyone to wake up to this fact. For there are many souls coming into the world today with a purpose that entails nothing less than preserving the planet for generations to come. And this is essential for each and every one of you.

It has been said (by Gary Zukav and others) that one cannot participate in the cause of anything without also participating in the result. And so it is that parents today, and their entire generation as well, have a contract to fulfill. And that is to enable this planetary regeneration. This is your participation in the cause, as it were. A sowing of seeds that you yourself will reap one day. And it makes nurturing the soul of every child that comes with this purpose a fundamental requirement and responsibility for all of you—parents and those of you who do not see that you are parents of a kind to these children as well.

Think of yourselves as elders or Godparents or great humanitarians in disguise—whatever it takes to do the work that is at hand, begin it. Make a difference in at least one child's life no matter who you are, for in doing so, you and the whole of humanity have everything to gain. And that is the gift of life itself.

Indeed, life on earth is a precious and holy thing. And all too many of you have forgotten this truth.It is time to remember. For your children. And for yourselves.

Two

To Nurture the Soul of a Child Is to Create a More Inspired World

FOR THE MOST part, most parents truly love their children dearly. But it is not always the case that they recognize or even concern themselves with the soul purpose of a child or what it is that child has come into the world to become.

This was not always the case. And even today, there are those cultures in which the ancient ways are still practiced, in which the entire village or tribe addresses this question, acknowledges the child's gift and supports his or her development with that unique purpose in mind, as it is seen as a great benefit to all. And indeed it is.

This is something we would encourage all parents to do. And to the extent that it becomes something entire families and extended families can participate in, we encourage that as well.

But to do this in a way that is meaningful, anyone who would participate must be willing to contemplate the nature of soul. How is it distinct from the personality? What are the ways one encourages a child to live with authenticity such that the personality is evolving in harmony with the soul?

In modern society, there is little that encourages or supports this kind of understanding. And while religions may touch on the subject, there is more wisdom to be found in the ancient ways of indigenous peoples with regard to this particular area of life. Poets and students of Jungian psychology know this. In fact, many have addressed the notion of what's lacking in modern culture very articulately. Rites of passage, initiation rituals and the mentoring of elders all do much to support children in a way modern society does not.

Instead, children are fed information continually, with nothing that serves to give them an orientation or a basis for evaluation of what they are continually bombarded with (more than any generation that has gone before them).

And yet in the midst of all this, people have the audacity to declare themselves proponents of family values and to debate the same in political arenas in which they of course fail to address what it is they fail to comprehend to begin with. In fact, it is quite a deplorable mess. And it is a poor substitute for the wisdom of the ages, the ancient spiritual teachings—indeed, simply entertaining the important questions with a sincere heart.

There is a reason teen suicide is at an all-time high. There is a reason children are shooting up the playground. There is a reason children are killing other children. And it is not that more of their mothers now work. It is that no one really takes the sacred contract seriously. And only a few even recognize that such a thing exists.

If one does recognize this truth, if one does take

it to heart, the Mother Teresas of the world will not be so rare and exceptional. Mother Teresa, like Christ, showed you the potential that is in you all.

Now this is not to say that everyone will, or even should, dedicate themselves exclusively to serving others in the way they did. But one can aspire to do what they did wherever and whenever it is possible to do so. One can look for and, indeed, begin to see the opportunities everywhere to make a difference in a child's life. To do something that truly supports them in the great souls they are and the persons they would become.

Loving attention, the care of the soul and spirit—not just the body or the developing mind—the recognition of one's gifts and purpose and dream and all manner of support in pursuing these things—this is what is required. And this has been said by many before. Their words are not merely beautiful quotations to call up on special occasions or grace the front of greeting cards. They are meant to be lived.

And, if they are to be lived—if, indeed, such things are to be accomplished—it will take everyone.

There is a primary role of mother. There is a primary role of father, which many a man is rediscovering. There is a role for grandparents and aunts and uncles. Family friends. Elders in the community. The masters and teachers of all disciplines. And yes, sports heroes are, indeed, role models. But they are not the only ones. Every person is a role model in the sense that they have an influence on the very young by the fact of their very presence in the world.

But it is the spiritual teachers who are needed most of all. Those who understand the nature of the soul journey, those who can be as a Yoda for every Luke Skywalker, from early on. And gender is not at issue here. For such is the dream of every child that it needs support to grow and flourish just as a flower needs sun and rain to bloom.

Think on the vision quest. For that is the journey that each is on. And though it may look different from one culture to the next, it is something to be reckoned with. If nurtured, it manifests in such a way as to support everyone. If ignored, it manifests as well, but in a form that all too often takes a great toll.

Look at the gangs in your cities. And they harm they do. Then ask yourself what you have to do with this. For it is the case that most of you participate in the cause whether you are aware of it or not, and so, to the same extent, you experience the result.

This is not something you can really ignore simply because it is your choice to do so. This is to invite life to remind you in a more powerful way, do you see? It is not a simple matter of turning off the news because it disturbs you. One who has a sacred obligation will be continually invited to fulfill it. With awareness. Or not. With pain. Or not. Do you not see this phenomenon at work each and every day?

This is what we would ask you all to wake up to. Become aware that you are, all of you together, continually re-creating the world in which you live. And that as powerful co-creators, there is really nothing you can ignore—least of all your children.

Begin to see the opportunities that will, indeed, present themselves to you to do things differently, to respond with a new awareness. Be willing to entertain the perspective of soul. And what is required will show itself to you. Begin to see what it is you have to give that is inspired in the moment, that is truly your gift to give, that may be as unconventional as anything you have ever done.

For whether you are a parent or a godparent by your own choice, you will be fulfilled in your giving in a way you have not been before. And in the moment of giving with a sincere heart, you shall receive all manner of blessings. And few experience a more joyful blessing than that of a child.

Three
Every Child Is an Awakening

Truly I say unto you, whoever does not receive the Kingdom of God like a child shall not enter therein.

Luke 18: 17

MANY, MANY things are said in the name of children, many promises are made, many ideals are put forth as to what must be done and who we must be to further life on the planet for those who will come after us, that never come to pass.

This is not because those who put forth such intentions are insincere. Nor is it because their words or their visions fail to inspire all of humanity. The reason such things do not come to pass is that so very many of you are not willing to make the changes that are required in your daily lives that facilitate, that bring about, that truly empower and enable another way of life, another way of being.

This is to say that the force of inertia proves formidable. This is to say that habit at the cultural level is not easily overcome. This is to say that what inspires in one moment is forgotten in the next. And that people, all too often, succumb to the belief that the opportunities for change presented with all manner of optimism and ingenuity are, in reality, insurmountable challenges that one cannot accomplish alone.

And it is precisely this idea of "alone" that prevents you from even making the attempt to live in a way that furthers the hopes and dreams of everyone—especially your youngest dreamers.

In the idea of aloneness and separation a kind of resignation sets in that is most difficult to dislodge. And it serves to keep an entire society from moving forward because this resignation—indeed cynicism—is so pervasive. It is the conviction of so many individuals within the culture, whether they are aware of it or not.

There is only one way to respond to this. And that is for each and every one of you to examine what is in your own hearts and minds and souls, and to ask yourself if it is worth the trouble to make these dreams a reality.

Indeed, it is most worthwhile to share such an examination, to explore these fundamental questions with other parents and other people who assume primary responsibilities for the care of children in your society. You are going to have to get involved with others to explore new options. As difficult as it may be to make time for this, very few things are a more valuable use of time. If you need to reevaluate your priorities in order to create opportunities to explore these questions, so be it.

For your reality is not fixed, it is fluid. It is not predestined, it is co-created. It is not mandated by God, but designed by each of you as you live each moment with the power to create as the Creator does—although you do not recognize this truth. And so you create unconsciously, half-heartedly—or worse, maintain the status quo by virtue of your belief that there is no other option and that you might as well face that fact.

This is the Godless society. This is the hell you create for yourselves. This is the basis for a great deal of suffering in the world that does not have to be. And it is this hopelessness and cynicism that is so pervasive that makes each of you feel so very powerless to do anything but resign yourselves to accepting the prevailing untruth, which perpetuates the cycle of despair itself. Do you see?

Futhermore, this is what you teach your children to believe in, to face up to, to accept as reality. And then you wonder why, today, even your children—the means to hope for you all—are in such despair.

This is to sacrifice your sons and daughters to the false beliefs of generations. This is to put them in harm's way—for you ask them to give their lives to perpetuate your way of life and everything you believe in. And it is in no way a reflection of the truth.

The truth is that your children are not of this world. They are the holy expression of the Divine Self, as you yourself are. And they would live in a greater awareness of this than you have, for that is the true nature of evolution. That is why they are here.

It is children who remind you what it is to be alive. It is children who remind you what it is to dream. It is children who remind you what it is to know the truth in your own heart. And yet it is the children you ignore, even as you would do that which you think is best for them.

You have a movie called *Big* in which a child brings magic to a grown-up world. This, indeed, occurs all around you, in every moment of every day. But how many of you see it, nurture it or even stop what you are doing for one moment to acknowledge and appreciate a dazzling and profound insight that is offered to you by one who has not yet forgotten who they are?

Most of you are continually unable to receive this gift of awareness. And those that do, those who share the experience, are seen as less than practical in their so-called naiveté. And that, as we would assure you, is to miss the point entirely. It is to turn your back on the divine blessings that renew the world in each moment in the spirit of children.

This is no fairy tale. It is how things work.

So look to the children in your life, in your care or in your world with eyes that can see. And they will show you another way.

Do not discourage their wisdom, do not deny their dreams. They are, indeed, life's longing for itself. And they are not to be led astray. Instead, enable them to follow the path of their own choosing, enable them to live their dreams. And, most of all, love them for the gifts they bring and not because they perpetuate some part of you.

Open your hearts. Open your eyes. And you will see a new world in the making. One that will come to pass with or without your consent.

When you find yourself ignoring the questions children put to you, stop yourself and entertain their concerns with a sincere heart. When you find yourself rushing through a day on automatic pilot—at home or at school or in the halls of a hospital—stop yourself. And be willing to be inspired by something, guided by something that comes to you in the words or song or story of a child. Relish it. Explore it. Expand on it and forget the stock answers you have always had for such questions.

Contemplate these things in your heart and your children will reveal a world to you that you have forgotten. A world in which you once lived. And that is one in which an open heart reveals another way to be, choices that are not evident otherwise, inspiration that speaks in the still small voice you are so often unable to hear.

Surrender your ideas of what a parent or teacher or caregiver should be and allow this process of interaction with awareness and an open heart to guide you.

The children will inspire you, they will help to heal your own childhood wounds. And in living in this exchange, you will see clearly where soul would take you.

Engage in the dance. Allow that the child is an equal partner, though it may not look that way. And they will show you what it is they need from you. Something that, at any given moment, may not be at all what you would think or even what the grown-up mind can fathom.

Things will become obvious to you that you have not seen before if you engage with children in this way.

If you choose to nurture the ways of soul, if you choose compassion, love and wisdom, you will do much to bring about peace for everyone.

If you perpetuate unconsciousness and despair, however, that will become both your legacy and your inheritance for generations to come.

You have so much, all of you, to give your children, to give all the children of the world. And you cannot begin it a moment too soon. It is long, long overdue in your world of broken promises and forsaken dreams.

Four

Parents and Children Are Dependent on Each Other

WHAT APPEARS TO be a dependence of children on their parents for survival is, in fact, a two-way street. For just as human beings are not self-reliant in their early years, no one is entirely self-reliant at any age.

Furthermore, the entire human race is quite dependent on its children not only for the continuation of human life, but for the opportunity they themselves will require to return again and again to complete their task. And so it is with everyone.

The ultimate task is to bring the soul awareness into being, into full expression in the world. And there is not one of you who can do that without another.

This is one of the ways the fact that you are all connected—are all one, and one with God—is manifest in your world.

And so to be parent or child is doing God's work. To live with a purpose of creating for another all that one would desire for oneself is a divine purpose. To live in awareness of this and with a wholehearted commitment to it is indeed to live in grace.

For when one is in harmony with this larger purpose of the Divine and the Divine within you all, the entire process of life is filled with more harmony, more love, more compassion. And all of these things make for a world which is indeed a reflection of soul, a manifestation of spirit made flesh. Or, in other words, this is what the world becomes when we, all of us, live from this highest awareness.

Now, since this is likely not your experience at present, your next question might well be "What am I to do to reconcile my present reality with this greater possibility?" And in this you can take heart. For in asking sincerely, it is given to you—life will conspire to show you the way.

You may see a dream in your child that calls you to be another way, in order to further that dream. You may see that a parent bestowed on you something that now comes to fruition in your own children. You may be called to do something that extends to your children, and to other children as well, the first step in changing their world in some way as to accommodate a larger perspective. If something is lacking, supply it. If something is limiting, transcend and transform it. If something is causing pain, love and release it for healing to occur.

Take these many and small steps, one at a time, all of you who are parents and who are not, and the world you create will begin more closely to resemble a world in which your soul can thrive. For indeed, such a world originates in soul awareness and cultivates those qualities of love and compassion that are nurturing of the authentic soul self in everyone.

Look around you. Wake up to your own soul, that divine seeker within you, and you will find much to do that heals, that lifts, that fulfills you in a way nothing else can. And let that activity, that purpose that rewards you, be a child's gift to you. For there is none greater. In honoring that which your children and all children inspire in you, you honor yourself, your soul, your God. And you make the world one in which there is always hope—something that would appear to be in short supply today.

But nothing could be further from the truth. For at any time, there is a choice to be made that takes you in the direction of greater awareness, and whenever you choose it, hope is born again and again and again. And you have only to look into the eyes of a child to see it.

This is what it means to make the world a better place for your children—to nurture the things of the soul, to create truth and love and joy in each "now" moment.

It is not enough to feed and clothe their bodies and educate their minds. One must honor their magnificent and powerful souls that are coming into being and always, always coming into being with much to give, each and every one.

Simon Birch (from the movie of the same name) is not alone in this. It is the case with every child. And to do less than honor this, to do less than provide for every child, is to forsake everything the world can be and become.

It is to forget why you are really here. All of you. It is to forget what the entire Universe is about,and that is light and love for everyone.

Christ (Jesus) calls Himself the Light of the world, but He also tells his disciples that they too are the Light of the world.

Joel Goldsmith*

And so are you.

* *The Infinite Way* (Marina del Rey, Calif.: DeVorss Publications, 1956) p. 55.

Five

As God Is like a Parent, So a Parent Is like a God

THE INTERDEPENDENCE OF all human life, indeed, all of life, is the foundation for all that is manifest in the physical world.

This interdependence is not just a scientific principle or an observable law of ecology, it is a spiritual truth. And, as a spiritual truth, it is something that many people grasp to varying degrees, but something few people live by in a way that is fully conscious.

If it were fully conscious, totally understood in human awareness, one would see that separation is an illusion. One would see that to perceive another as better than or less than oneself is an illusion. One would see that, as Joel Goldsmith put it, you are like a wave on the ocean that cannot be separated from the next wave or, indeed, the ocean itself.

So this being ultimate reality, how does one live in this awareness with regard to children?

To begin with, one no longer sees them as powerless or "less than," though this may look another way. In addition, one does not look to them to fulfill that which is illusion. And that includes any idea that they are your possession or any notions of ego that have to do with living out your dream or carrying on a family tradition or bearing all responsibility for the perpetuation of your particular genetic package.

It means granting them the freedom that you yourself desire. That every person desires—freedom from oppression in any form.

This is not to say you disregard their welfare or expect them to be more self-reliant than they are, for, as children, there is much they require of you, as we have stated.

What it means is that you do not impose expectations of who they will become that are inconsistent with who they are.

It means loving them for who they are rather than demanding they earn that love by acquiescing in any arbitrary wishes on your part—and arbitrary is the key here.

Every parent has things to teach a child about making their way in the world and how to avoid coming to harm (avoiding the hot stove, for example). But there is much in the way of expectation that is placed upon children that is not the least bit appropriate and does not begin to take into account who they are.

These are the so-called conventions of life. The footsteps one is required to follow that have led you all astray. And yet you insist your children will be disadvantaged if they do not do the same.

And so you strive to raise your children in the same way, to educate them in the same way, to standardized their experiences in terms of common denominators that are grounded in misconceptions and illusions.

The common ground is that of the spirit or soul, and there are things that nurture its expression, as well as those things that suffocate the spirit.

But once it is allowed to emerge, the spirit of any child is going to require quite different things in order to further its development, its success in the world, than that of any other child. And so to seek to standardize child care and education and even methods of parenting is to encourage one to disregard what is standing before them, and that is a child with very individual requirements.

As you can see, the paradox is that while all are one and there is no separation between you, the nature of the individual soul is unique. There is common ground for everyone, and yet each of you comes into the world with a unique purpose and a unique gift. And not only is this uniqueness not fully recognized or appreciated at a cultural level, it is not supported to any great extent in your institutions which standardize without regard either to what is unique or even to what is truly the common ground or common experience, which has at its center a spiritual reality.

This is not an argument for prayer in the schools, either. For what prayer would satisfy those of many faiths?

Rather, it is to say that if one takes the question of what it is to honor our sacred contract with children to the level of those cultural institutions that are co-created by all of you, one will see quickly how much they fail to allow for individual development, how much they in fact suppress what is unique, authentic and inspired in every child, and how much this subject of education is really something to look at in an entirely different light.

As well, there are many other things that need to be reevaluated in this way. Just about everything in mass culture, for example.

The great advantage of such reexamination, however, is that you are living at a time when many things are possible that were not possible not so long ago. And it is indeed the case that the level of technology available to individuals in modern Western society has at its core the potential for meeting individual needs in a way your institutions, by their very nature, are not capable of. Yet technology alone is not the answer, but rather technology as a tool that enables every parent, every teacher, every mentor of every kind a way to shift their attention from what is called rote learning to a form of education that is totally individualized and operates at the level of authentic empowerment.

To do this and to see that education is not confined to schoolrooms or so many hours in a day is to engage in, to begin to create, an environment and, indeed, the methods which truly nurture all children in ways that really count. That allow them to explore their dreams and, yes, to explore anything it is their wish to explore—without sacrificing their sense of wonder, their natural curiosity, their spontaneous and generous and totally unique spirits in the process.

And that is the goal when one is conscious and living in awareness—the freedom to actualize the Self. It is the reason you are here. The reason you are alive. And it is nothing less than an expression of God, of All That Is in its infinite fullness and ever-increasing richness. For though you are as one, no one of you is exactly like another. And each one is to be loved and nurtured and recognized and appreciated in order for God, the Universe, the All in All to know itself in its entirety.

The ways of the world could reflect this far more than they do. And all that is really required for this to happen is being awake. Indeed, that is what the New Millennium is all about.

Six

Be Clear about Your Intentions, For They Are Crystal Clear to Your Children

THE DEGREE TO which any two people—but especially parents and their children—have been around before has much to do with how well they are able to nurture the soul purpose. It is a knowing that carries over from lifetime to lifetime And that is why there is often a sense that one truly knows what is best for a child without doing the work of engaging with this question of purpose that encourages the child to participate in the process.

However, there is no small danger here. And the danger is what we would call interfering with another's choosing.

This is something many parents and, especially those with a great degree of authentic knowing, feel they have every right to do. And they can be quite adamant about it. But this is not appropriate in any circumstance. And it can be as much of a set back as if there were no awareness or intuitive knowledge of the child operating at all.

It is respecting this god self of another and its sovereignty, its sacredness of purpose, its freedom of will and choice that is at all times required. This is something you, as a parent, will need to remind yourself again and again.

And when it is not the case, when parents assert

their will over a child's and are disrespectful of the sovereignty, the most bitter conflicts arise. And a process of estrangement begins that may not reverse itself in this lifetime.

There is, by the way, much in certain cultural traditions that supports this, that is in error in assigning this as a responsibility to parents. And, in fact, those who have recognized this and broken with such traditions have been misunderstood and blamed for so-called permissiveness. Dr. Spock was one.

He was among the first to make a departure from unnecessarily restrictive traditions in parenting. And much of his work was inspired by a strong sense of respect for what the child's needs are, as opposed to what is convenient for the parent. Or what is useful to a cultural or social system that would have the individual in service to itself, as opposed to living an authentic and inspired life.

It is no accident his influence was so pervasive at a time when most of you who are now parents were coming into the world. For you are preparing the way for great changes which will manifest in the world as your own children come into the fullness and maturity of their own lives.

Each generation prepares the way for the next. And while every soul participates at the level of individual goals and purpose, so each comes with something to give: a gift of awareness, of soul, a contribution that it is no one's place to reject or to deprive them of—and that is precisely what occurs when, in error, a parent interferes with the child's own choosing.

Imagine, at such times that you are tempted to do this, that your roles are reversed and that it is you who would choose for yourself, as would the child before you. We think you will see in an instant what is appropriate, that in your heart of hearts you will know the right thing to do. Know also, that in granting another their freedom to choose, you are granting yourself that freedom as well. For, as we cannot say enough, what goes around comes around. And yes, you will find yourself on the receiving end of all you have created.

Now, lest you fear the mistakes you will make that are inevitable because you are human, realize that intention is the key here. If, as a parent or mentor or teacher, your intentions are, in fact, to honor the sovereign soul, and to further the divine purpose in another, and to respect their choosing, that is what your words and actions will reflect. You needn't walk on egg shells or avoid being firm in your decisions where it is appropriate for you to do so.

But always, always, be aware of what is operating in your own heart, be diligent with regard to your intentions and seek to live with integrity, as one who has resolved many of the inconsistencies and contradictions between what is true in your heart and how you are living your life day to day. Only then will children have the respect for you and any decisions you would impose on them, at any age—which otherwise you may well demand, but to no avail.

There is a wisdom, a knowing, in every soul, at any age. And if you are operating without integrity, if your intentions are less than honorable, your children will know this. Your partner will know this. Your dog will know this.

Do everything in your power to know what is in your own heart before you would ask anyone to live by what you would assert as truth at any level. It is in your own best interest to do so.

Seven
Acknowledge that Children Have a Powerful Knowing Most of You Have Lost Touch With

THE FIRST THING TO remember, always, about children is that they have an innocence you do not.

This is to say that children have not yet entirely forgotten who they are, that children are more in touch with their own wisdom, their own intuitive powers and the God self or soul within.

This is what makes them so gifted at offering up insightful and, at times, provocative statements as to what they observe in you and in the world of adults, in general, with regard to all the evasive maneuvering and avoidance of what, to them, is obvious truth.

This is their great gift to the world and it is their great vulnerability also. And this vulnerability is twofold. The first aspect has to do with the fact that most people are uncomfortable with the obvious truth and that is why they learn to avoid it. It makes demands of them they don't wish to explore. And, in their defensive posturing, they may retaliate in a way that is quite harmful to the innocent.

All manner of retaliation occurs, from that which is called child abuse to the more subtle forms of disempowerment that encourage children to deny their truth, their knowing, their souls. Much harm is done, much that serves to erode the sense of authentic self that is everyone's birthright.

The other form of retaliation that is equally damaging is that having to do with the exploitation of their powerlessness—not in the sense of authentic (soul) power, but in the sense that they are granted no power relative to others or even over their own lives by the adults entrusted with their care and well-being. This is to say children are granted no authority, they are not recognized as having any rights and they are often oppressed by the very people who are said to have their best interests at heart.

It is time to change this. Time to reevaluate every assumption about what is in the best interests of your children. For much that is endorsed as legitimate in this way is based on illusion, based on nothing that serves the spirit, nothing that honors the soul. Much harm is done with little awareness of the far-reaching and, eventually, self-perpetuating consequences of such behavior.

Now perhaps this suggests to you a need to start over—that none of your methods and institutions can withstand this kind of reevaluation. But this is not entirely true. There is much that can be salvaged. And, in engaging in a reevaluation such as this, what you are likely to see is that there are those in the world doing much to transform your institutions, those who are doing much that truly does serve the best interests of your children *in spite of the constraints of the systems they are working in.*

A dialogue with individuals such as these is in order so that you may renew your social forms in everything from parenting to public education to community service. Reform is imperative. Reform is overdue. One must be willing to overhaul the system such that it serves the authentic needs of children and not the agendas of those who are either in control of that system or dependent on it for their own personal gain.

This will not be easy. And we must tell you that it will require the highest level of integrity from any who would participate, in order for this to amount to anything more than a mere exercise in frustration. But it must be done.

It is a requirement for all that will emerge as a result of the paradigm shift your world is now in. Your institutions will but renew themselves or fall away. Your intentions to reform them must be carried out and not merely debated. And your politicians are not the ones to do this.

Every one of you must be willing to take on some responsibility here. Parents need to work with other parents. Parents need to work with teachers. The true leaders within your communities need to work with those in control of your institutions or they will in no way address what is critical to the community of children—which is quite under represented in your power structures.

Do this work. Engage others in the dialogue. And, most of all, engage in the soul-searching that is a prerequisite for discernment regarding what it is you would create.

Make a time for reflection each day. It doesn't have to be long, but if you are consistent, you will begin to open yourself to intuitive guidance. In these moments of silence, you may begin, again, to hear the still small voice within. And you will find that you are able to contemplate things in the heart and not the head.

Make the inspiration you find there what you share. Make this the direction you move in—there are answers to life's problems and challenges within you all, if you but go there. Willingly. Earnestly. Openly. This is not so difficult.

Ground yourself in the authentic. That is to say, learn to distinguish your own ego impulses from those intentions that are inspired by a greater awareness of the greater good. The oneness you all are. And yes, be willing to put yourself in another's place—in this case any child's—and ask what you yourself would want in your heart of hearts. Recognize that what nurtures another will nurture you in ways you haven't yet imagined.

That is because, in spiritual reality, you are both one. And it is the divine creator within you that would express itself, experience itself, and lead you all to more joy, more compassion, more love in every aspect of your lives and, especially, wherever children are concerned. For they are more aware, more open and totally in touch with their inspiration and its source within them. They are not yet blocked and burdened as so many of you are.

Open your heart. Honor your commitment to every child, not just your own. And allow for the guidance that will come to you when your intention is to do that which is truly best for them—which may not look at all like what the culture has endorsed heretofore.

> *Have you never read "Out of the mouth of babes and sucklings thou hast brought perfect praise"?*
>
> Matthew 21:16

Be aware that old forms will fall away in order for new forms to be born. And know that your children will have much to teach you along the way. Most of all, expand your dialogue with them. And from the mouths of babes you will hear such wisdom that you will know in your hearts what is right to do.

The task at hand awaits you. Put aside your doubts and fears, put aside your need for absolute certainty and predictability and control and comfort with all that is familiar and explore. There is much that awaits you, much that is as a great longing in the hearts of many that will do no less than transform your lives and your world, it you but bring it forth.

Eight

Your Children Are Showing You the Way to a World That's Meant to Be

When does a child come of age? And is the soul awareness they brought with them intact when they do? This might be a way to evaluate whether you are serving their needs or not. Whether you are enabling them to bring forth what is within them or not. Whether your best intentions are honoring their souls or not.

If it is the case, you will not have to ask. It will be as obvious to you as the difference between night and day. And it will bring great joy to their lives. And to yours.

If it is not the case, you will find you have much work to do in reexamining and reevaluating all that you have done or not done to honor the sacred contract between you.

Consider your so-called failures as great opportunities to learn. Work with others who share your intentions to lay the groundwork for a new understanding of what it means to raise children in a way that honors who they are over who you want them to be. For in granting them this freedom, and in supporting them in bringing forth a life purpose and a soul dream that is completely authentic, you will have discovered one of the most powerful forces for change on the planet. And that is what it truly means to serve another, to serve the highest common good.

This is the goal of every relationship. But it is

nowhere more important than with those innocent souls who continually bless the world in their knowingness, their freshness of spirit and their innate desire to live in truth and love.

Hate is not born in them, it is learned. Separation is not born in them, it is learned. Powerlessness is not born in them, it is learned. And when you cease to teach these things to your children, you will, indeed, learn that the truth shall set them—and you—free.

Free to create a world in which all people are acknowledged, all people are supported, all people are aware of what they are here to give. And that is love in its infinite varieties.

Be it love as expressed in music or poetry, love as expressed in healing or love as expressed in living in harmony with each other and with nature. The ways to express love are infinite in their variety. And they are what make human life so compelling a way to bring forth what the soul desires to know and to experience—beauty, joy, wonder and all the subtle meanings of each of these that fill the heart and join each heart to another and another and another.

This is the gift all of you have for one another, though you know it not. You are all a part of God experiencing itself—this is what is meant by spirit made flesh. This is what you come here for. And if you do not understand this, it is because you have lost the wisdom you brought with you into this world and have not yet found it back again.

And for most of you, it is the suffering in your childhood, in your innocence, that caused you to lose this powerful knowing within. Anything you do—indeed, everything you do from then on is about getting this back whether you are conscious of it or not. You may look for it outside yourself. You may seek it in another. You may seek it in every worldly thing you have created for your own distraction. But you can only find it within you.

This is the human experience, but it does not have to be so. For if one lives with the awareness of what a child brings into the world and helps them to preserve it, to live it, you create an entirely new world of possibility for each and every one of you.

This is the task at hand. It is time to begin it now. For in such a way are you meant to redeem your souls and preserve the planet. In such a way are you to bring on what is called the New Millennium, in which peace and a fullness of spirit will reign.

This second coming is to discover that which is the Christ consciousness in you. And your children will be the ones who show you the way. For many of them are coming here precisely with this purpose and to see this become an earthly reality in their time.

For that to happen, much will fall away. For that to happen, every one of you must become more aware. For that to happen, you must honor the sacred contract, the soul agreements you all have with the children of the world, the whole of the next generation, and the fulfillment of your promise for all of humanity.

Avoid the constant temptation to unconsciously repeat the patterns of your own upbringing. Look beyond the so-called expert opinions prevalent in mass consciousness. And seek to expand your understanding of who any child is—for, indeed, children come here with their own magnificent souls intact. You do not have to fill them up or make them your own. You have only to be awake and fully present and open your heart.

Things are changing rapidly in your world. And if you do not hold fast to these truths, you will find it all too easy to lose your way. There is nothing to be gained in remaining unconscious. There is no bliss to be found in ignorance, as it were. And there is no small danger in assuming others will take the responsibility, others—those vocal and misguided proponents of the status quo—who are all too often "full of passionate intensity, while the best lack all conviction," to quote Yeats.

If you are aware, on the other hand, if you are in touch with the wisdom of your own soul and the truth that is in your own heart, if you are allowing yourself to be guided into the new world that is being born through your children, you will live to see things you never thought could be. And that is what you signed on for, so to speak.

Do not fear what is coming to pass before your very eyes, but embrace these changes, welcome them. They shall bring about everything you have longed for throughout your human history. An end to war.

And disease. And famine. An end to hatred and oppression of any kind. An end to the destruction of nature and the many creatures who constitute your absolute delight in the natural world.

These are the things you shall, many of you, come to see in your lifetime. And this is where your children shall live, if you but prepare them for it in a way that honors their souls. They are little gods who have much to teach you all. And so begin it.

Open yourself up to all that is meant to be. Surrender every idea you have ever had about what it is to be a good parent and what really nurtures. Consider who it is that is in control here and who it is that is the true parent, the spiritual parent, the divine parent within you.

Discover your own vulnerable, wounded heart and a higher self that will guide you. An authentic self that has been both parent and child more times than you can know. One who chose to participate in the world in this way and has every angel and teacher and unseen guardian of the light in your corner.

There is nothing you do alone. And there is always, always much divine assistance available to anyone who has chosen to prepare the way for another. And if ever you doubt what you are doing or who you must become, the children shall be your constant reminders in this redemption of the world and everything in it.

Nine

Reevaluating Accepted Notions of Parenting Is in Order

WHETHER YOU HAVE your own children, have adopted children or have no children at all, you have a part to play in how the world supports them or fails to support them in their coming into awareness of what is in their souls.

The task at hand is to shift paradigms and to further, in every way, everything these divine beings (like all of you) are coming into this world to do.

It is more important than ever that they be nurtured in such a way as to accomplish this task of renewing the planet and preserving the potential for life here for generations to come. Your assistance is critical. And it is time to dispense with anything that is in the way of this and to do the hard work of reevaluating and restructuring your social and cultural institutions that currently do more to limit a child's potential than to further it. (The Waldorf schools and those few remaining indigenous cultures in which the elders are responsible for child raising are an exception to this.)

Parents must begin to work with other parents, to support each other in exploring what it means to parent in a way that furthers the social transformation. And there is much to be learned from the ancient ways and wisdom of indigenous peoples that can be helpful in this.

This process is not unlike women's consciousness-raising groups that arose in the Sixties and Seventies. And yet the need for fathers to participate equally should be quite obvious. Though they may in many cases feel somewhat less inclined to nurture their children in this way, given generations of conditioning that come to rest upon you all.

But the fact that fathers haven't played as active a role is part of the problem here. Robert Bly, Dan Millman, David Spangler and others have much to offer on the subject of a father's role—and a father's absence. In addition, Marc Bryan's *The Prodigal Father* gives hope to those fathers who have not been a participant in their children's lives and offers ways to change this.

Women, on the other hand, more typically bearing primary responsibility for the care of children and therefore more willing to engage with these questions, must begin to get more clear with regard to their priorities. With two-thirds of mothers working today, this is no small task.

Support from others—other parents and those within your family, extended family, friends and so-called vertical community—is going to be completely necessary here. For you are, in a sense, trying to recreate the village, as it were. To recreate community in a new way and to foster the support for yourselves and your children that represents your highest ideals. Nothing short of this will do.

Some "rocking of the boat" is definitely in order for those of you whose employers don't clearly support your primary parental role in every way that they could. And you are going to have to insist on these things, demand changes that will not come easily—there is simply far too much at stake.

Yet if everyone wakes up, if everyone does this, you will not be alone, and indeed this task will be much easier than if you try to go it alone in modern "superwoman" fashion.

There is also a role for those single people in your life and those friends who do not have children, who are, perhaps all too often, excluded from your circle. They have much to offer you and your children in the way of both support and the enrichment of your day-to-day lives.

Be open to this. Make the effort more than most of you have done. These are the ways reassessing your priorities will help you to see that not only is there a necessity for people to come together, there is everything to be gained here.

The amazing thing is that so very many options are open to all of you that you have never even thought about before, let alone explored. And for no good reason at all.

And while it may be true there may well be those who have chosen to remove themselves from your life or limit your relationship in many ways as a result of your role as a parent, it is also true that many who can and would support you are not invited in.

Extend the opportunity to them. You will know by their pleasure at this that, indeed, there is room for more love in your life that is already so full. For every person who is irritated or annoyed with your diminishing availability to them because of your role as a parent, there are two or three or five others who welcome participation.

These are the ones to encourage. These are the ones who will transform, along with you, a culture that excludes children in a kind of false culture into a culture that supports them in every way. You will know them by their willingness, you will know them by the way they connect with a child, you will know them by their quality of heart.

Look with new eyes. Open up to all the possibilities. Prepare to enrich your own life and each life that touches yours as you take up this task of providing real opportunity for every child, real support for their goals and dreams, instead of all that passes for it now, all that shuts down the sense of Self that is within them, not to mention their natural curiosity about the world. Yes—learning curves shoot up and then sharply decline in the early elementary grades. Doesn't this tell you something?

You push your children to succeed within the context of one badly designed educational model and then wonder why they hate school, why test scores are in decline, why "dumbth" is on the rise. Many, many things must change if you are to *begin* to provide children with anything that furthers their purpose, that assists them in accomplishing all the things they are here to do.

And the very thing that you most fail to provide, that you fail to provide because many of you who are parents have not yet acquired it for yourselves, is that body of knowledge that only the wisest among you can provide.

They may be elders among you. They may be your artists and poets and the great thinkers among you. In any case, chances are they have been relegated to working on the fringes of your youth-oriented culture, receiving little in the way of acknowledgment, much less support, for all they have to contribute to your way of life.

There are wise ones among you. Seek them out. But do not expect that they will necessarily fit your pictures. And recognize that, unlike those who would proclaim their own righteousness and wisdom, the wisest among you will also be the most humble.

Develop the ability, individually and collectively, to discern that which is authentic wisdom—that which opens up and expands your ability to create the highest reality one can choose to create—from those who call themselves wise but beg for a return to old ways (not to be confused with ancient ways of indigenous peoples) that have produced nothing that could be called an expansion of awareness.

Rather, the old ways of which these people are speaking are a return to those things which protect the vested interests of a privileged few and in no way serve the larger good. If you are in doubt, merely listen to your talk radio programs and you will know what we are talking about—those things that encourage division rather than unity among you.

In other words, become the "stable bow":

And a woman who held a babe against
her bosom said, Speak to us of Children.
And he said:
Your children are not your children.
They are the sons and daughters of Life's
longing for itself.
They come through you, but not from
you,
And though they are with you yet they
belong not to you.

You may give them your love but not
your thoughts.
For they have their own thoughts.
You may house their bodies but not
their souls,
For their souls dwell in the house of tomorrow,
which you cannot visit, not even
in your dreams.
You may strive to be like them, but seek
not to make them like you.
For life goes not backward nor tarries
with yesterday.

You are the bows from which your children
as living arrows are sent forth.
The archer sees the mark upon the path
of the infinite, and He bends you with His
might that His arrows may go swift and far.
Let your bending in the archer's hand
be for gladness;
For even as He loves the arrow that flies,
so He loves the bow that is stable.

Kahlil Gibran*

* From *The Prophet,* by Kahlil Gibran. Copyright 1923 by Kahlil Gibran and renewed 1951 by Administrators C T A of Kahlil Gibran Estate and Mary G. Gibran. Reprinted by permission of Alfred A. Knopf, a Division of Random House Inc.

Ten

The Future Is Quite Literally in Your Hands

THE REASON THAT so very many of you are threatened by the changes we are talking about here is that you feel you are being asked to explore unknown territory, and that you are being asked to relinquish a degree of control over your children that you feel is quite appropriate.

These things are an illusion. For, in truth, there are other ways known to be far more valuable to raising children who are self-empowered and self-aware. You have merely to rediscover them. They are the ancient ways of the village, in which the elders who have an understanding of the soul journey shape the day-to-day lives of the young in a way that truly nurtures the spirit within them, the god self, the soul. You must do your homework on this score, as it were.

As for the relinquishing of control—this, too, is an illusion. For though you may think you have the power to control another, in truth, you do not. It is merely the case that you are creating obstacles to their self-expression, which will always assert itself, but not always in the ways that are most beneficial.

It is the case that your interference, as it were, can merely direct this expression in ways that are either good for children and the culture or society of which they are a part or not. And attempts to control, to have your children live according to your will and not their own, can produce very negative results.

For this sets up an adversity and reinforces a sense of separation that invites them to undermine, to sabotage, to discreate all they will experience as limitation—and these are the very things you often would instill in them. So your desire for control is, in effect, counterproductive. It defeats the very purpose that is your intention. It fails by design.

Only in granting one the very freedom of self-determination that you yourself would claim can you live in harmony. (And this is true for all relationships with all people, not just those relationships you have with your children.)

Wise ones know this. Wise ones have the ability to offer guidance with unconditional love. Wise ones know what is required to further the highest expression of another, to enable young people to bring forth the best that is within them without interfering in their choices but instead by assisting them in learning more quickly, more effortlessly, from the choices they make.

Wise ones also inspire—which is to say they give children a living example of what one can be that allows a child to see the potential wisdom in the Self and bring it forth.

Parents are not necessarily able to do this. And you need only look around you to see who it is who is bringing children into the world in greater and greater numbers—they are increasingly the very young, the very poor, the most disempowered among you. This is not meant for you to judge them. But rather for you to begin to see that it is not wisdom you are passing on to your children.

It is, rather, the case that most of your children are being quite neglected in many, many ways. As Mother Teresa has said, "There are many kinds of poverty." There are children suffering in every way in your world. And yet most of you care not. When you do care, it is for those children you consider your own—and these you would mold into images of yourself, these you would see live out your wish, not their own, these you would offer the best of every material thing one can possess while all but starving their souls. This is the insanity of a mass culture that is based on illusion and, indeed, on the particular illusion that the Divine is external to you, outside of you. This is to say you do not recognize the divine becoming that is within each of you. And of those that do, you take little heed.

There are exceptions, to be sure. But they are just that—exceptions. The greatest number of you, by far, are quite unconscious as to what it is you are doing. And it is time to wake up.

Things are changing rapidly in your world. There is less predictability in your lives than ever before. And most of you cannot truly envision the world in which your children will live. This is terrifying for many of you, consciously or unconsciously. And, as you cannot control the future that is causing you greater and greater angst and uncertainty, many of you are trying to control your children. As a means of keeping them safe, at best. Or worse, as a means of feeling some kind of control—any kind of control—in your lives regardless of the cost.

It is time to see clearly that what is called for in your world is a new way of being, a new way of living, a new way of organizing yourselves that furthers the common good of all. This is the only way.

Some among you are already on this path. Others are holding the possibility and calling out to the rest. But until each of you is willing to become more aware, more conscious of the power you have within you to create that which you truly desire for yourselves and your children, your mass cultural beliefs will keep you stuck right where you are.

Be willing to let go of many of these notions of how things should be. Examine the larger questions. Be willing to be truly inspired to live another way. Be willing to be shown another way. Be open to the question, and life will offer up alternatives you didn't know existed. Life will offer up, will reveal to you, the many paths to wisdom that are all around you, but that most of you do not see. For within all of you, within each and every one, lie the seeds of your own awakening, your own divine becoming.

Surrender to the best that is within you—even if at this moment all you know of the best that is within you is that in seeking with a most sincere heart you shall find another way. Surrender your ideas of separation and judgment. Be willing to entertain the notion that you are all one and that the most essential truths, the authentic desires of another—that is to say the soul desires—are no different for anyone than they are for you. Though they are, indeed, expressed uniquely.

Discover your common ground and build on it. Begin to share your dreams, your desires, and above all your willingness to explore a larger vision together and to create a world that supports you all.

The alternative—maintaining the status quo—is no longer possible on your planet if you wish human life to continue in the long term. Push has come to shove, as it were.

Eleven

Open Your Hearts to the Children and They Will Show You Another Way

THERE ARE SO many subtleties, complexities and nuances that are continually exchanged between parents and their children—whether one is conscious of them or not—that it is very difficult to here address the specifics of any particular relationship of this sort.

What we would do in this forum is make a case for greater awareness and for living in the question "What does it mean to nurture and support another human being coming into this life?" As well as "What are those things in our collective experience, our social institutions that all of us would address in an effort to remove the limitations which we have been unconsciously perpetuating?" And "What are those things that we would consciously create that will do far more to inspire, enable and empower these children who have so much to give the world?"

If one wishes to, there are many ways to gain insight into their individual relationships. But it is these larger questions we would all of us do well to consider, to experiment with, to answer for ourselves and begin to apply if we are to turn things around in the world.

The time has come for the world to reflect a greater awareness, to provide every child with the opportunity not just to survive, to have enough to eat, but to thrive.

Look around you. How many of your children are thriving?

Do what you can do, individually and collectively, to make a difference. Whether your choice is to provide financial support for those in need of food and shelter and medicine, or a choice to transform your relationship with your own children and to work with other parents to improve your educational system. More than a few of you may consider adopting children. And there are many, many children who need homes. Be assured, if you make such a choice as this, the child who comes will have much to teach you, that children and their adoptive parents have no less powerful a connection between them than those who share a biological connection or blood tie.

And if your choice is to bring more wisdom into your parenting, into every child's life, begin to make that your conscious intention and much will come your way. Much guidance is available to any who would seek it out. However, seek it within also.

Pray to be open to a new way of seeing, of being. Pray to the god self within or to God, the Goddess, the Great Spirit—the point is, open yourself to divine guidance by whatever name you choose. And you will begin to find your way. For all of you are much supported by those who assist everyone in their soul journey. And every one of you has within you the power to create anything you wish.

The nature of creation is such that first you must

hold within you that which you would create. As within, so without.

So to make the kinds of changes we are talking about here, one must be willing to engage the question, live the question. As one is guided and develops a vision of what they would like to create or who they would like to be, they must hold that intention in their thoughts in order to bring it about. They must act with that intention in order to create from it. And, to the extent one is clear and fully aware, there is no reason you can't create what you dream of, your highest vision of what can be.

Furthermore, if many of you hold this higher vision, it will come to pass more quickly and for all of you. That is how you co-created the situations you presently find yourselves in. And that is how to begin to have something new, something that arises from your greater understanding of what you and your children are here to do, why you have chosen this particular adventure with each other.

Every time is characterized by particular challenges. And every period in human history has seen those who revealed a new way to their fellow human beings.

At this particular time, as the world grows into the so-called New Age, there is an opportunity, a requirement even, for many of you to participate at this higher level of awareness. And there are many, many teachers and teachings to draw upon.

But there is no more important truth than that which you find within you.

Discover what is in your own hearts. Be willing to live by your own highest principles. Be willing to reexamine everything you have ever been taught. And be willing to be inspired.

Allow for the vitality of children and the awareness they hold to reshape your consciousness and your world. Allow that there is wisdom in changing—indeed, breaking—some of the rules. Many of the rules. Allow that, as we have said, from the mouth of babes—and second-graders and teenagers and all those who are children by virtue of their dependence on you until a given age—a new world will begin to emerge. It is in them. They are the seeds. They are the evolution of your kind. They are the divine messengers every generation requires to see its way into a world that is yet in the making. They are your inspiration and your joy. They are your beloved children who are here to redeem the world from all the pain and suffering of unconscious creation and re-create it in the image of the Divine.

This is to say that your children are not your children, they are children of the Universe, the Father/Mother God, the Great Spirit that is awakening in the lives of everyone and is always, always generating a far greater love than the mortal self can fathom. Allow this tide of love to flood your world and everything in it. This is how all shall be healed. This is the great gift your children bring, if you but empower them and acknowledge their souls.

They are the reaching out from your present reality. They are the creators of the new. They are the way in which new dreams come to pass. They are the way in which the evolution of life on the planet and of the prevailing consciousness occurs. They are those who bring an increasing awareness and an increasing expression of that which is called the divine, that which is the cosmic consciousness that is ever unfolding. They bring you to another dimension of being which you, in turn, will inherit as the circle of life continues. This is the sacred circle of becoming that connects any lifetime to the next and the next and the next.

And the circle is now ascending as a spiral to a new level or dimension in which unity is coming into expression as the prevailing consciousness. And when unity is the prevailing consciousness, there will be peace in the world.

There is much to be done. Much that is begging for your mercy and your love. Become a light unto the darkness. Embrace all the children of the world. And they will show you another way. For, indeed, that is an aspect of the soul dream with which all of you have come.

Twelve

The Gift of Hope Is in the Children— All the Children

THE PURPOSE FOR which many of your children have, and are, coming to the planet is quite a grand vision. It is beyond a good many of you who are parents at this time, as it is beyond the level of understanding that predominates in your mass culture.

And yet if you were in touch with, truly aware of, what your own soul purposes are, you would share their visions. For indeed, all of you have, at the soul level, chosen to prepare the way. This is something all of you have chosen, as everyone who is ever born into this earth has also done.

For preparing the way is but one aspect of preserving life on the planet. And all of you have an interest in that, conscious or not.

What makes this particular time, and these particular children, and these particular questions we have engaged in more relevant than ever before is that most of you—and especially these children of the world today—do not want a repeat of the past destruction you have seen on this planet.

There is much in your mythology that tells you of past civilizations that were very advanced and yet destroyed themselves. And this is true. And so it is that many of you are choosing another way this time.

Because, indeed, as scientists and peacemakers

and any number of inspired messengers have been saying, you are on the brink once more. And quite capable of rendering the planet unfit for human life in the very immediate future.

But this is not to say that panic is in order. Rather, consciousness and cooperation are in order. And that is what this paradigm shift is all about.

It is about being aware that you are all one. And that God dwells within each of you and all of you. And in all things.

It is about devoting yourselves to creating that which you truly desire. And in truth, most of you long for another way but haven't made the effort to discover, much less create, it.

This calling—whether it comes to you through your children, through a book like this one and many others or through a personal epiphany—is to wake up, to become aware and to see where your soul would guide you and what it is you would do to realize (to make real) a new world order. Yes, you have heard these words before. And more than a few of you are frightened by them.

But this will come to pass. And the degree to which you embrace this for the good of all people, and the degree to which you grant your children the wisdom that nurtures, the freedom that inspires and the love that sustains *all* of them, is the degree to which you will realize your own soul's deep longing.

If this is something you would be absolutely certain of, look within your own heart. Do whatever you would do to find your own wisdom within you.

You are likely to discover that, indeed, you have not even begun to do the things you have dreamed of. Your children are a reminder. And they are not merely your children. They are the divine becoming. They have a gift for you all and you for them.

But if one does not recognize that this is so, the future does, indeed, look bleak. In fact, bleak doesn't begin to describe the means to your demise that is, as yet, entirely possible. And of your own making.

There are those who say that if God did not want you to do this or that He wouldn't have given you the means. What they fail to see is that God gave you the means to everything. And it is you who choose what you will create.

The choices before you now are as important as any you have ever had. Will you choose life for everyone? Will you choose a world in which every child grows in wisdom? Will you choose a world in which every one of you has the right to be all you would become? Will you choose to live from your highest intentions and visions? Or not?

There is so very much at stake. It is time for everyone to recognize this. To prepare the way. And let your children lead you to the very best vision of what human life can be.

This is their sacred purpose. And indeed, we would remind you that it was yours to assist and empower them. For so very, very many of you have entirely forgotten.

Your children are here to create peace for all people.

Your children are here to create harmony and balance in all things, to renew and to sustain life on the planet.

Your children are here to bring forth a vision of unity and to facilitate an evolution in consciousness that is beyond your imagining.

Surrender to the highest good for all of them and you will serve your own. For that is the truth of things, after all. We are all one.

If you can embrace this truth, in any form, you thus take the small step that is a giant step for all humankind. There is every reason for hope if you will do this. And that is why this message comes to you.

As once the winged energy of delight
carried you over childhood's dark abysses,
now beyond your own life build the great
arch of unimagined bridges.

Wonders happen if we can succeed
in passing through the harshest danger;
but only in a bright and purely granted
achievement can we realize the wonder.

To work with *Things in the indescribable*
relationship is not too hard for us;
the pattern grows more intricate and subtle,
and being swept along is not enough.

Take your practiced powers and stretch them out
until they span the chasm between two
contradictions . . . For the god
wants to know himself in you.

Rainer Maria Rilke*

* From *The Selected Poetry of Rainer Maria Rilke,* by Rainer Maria Rilke. Copyright © 1982 by Stephen Mitchell. Reprinted by Random House, Inc.

Book Three

SPIRITUAL COMMUNITY

The Transformation of the World through Soul Purpose

Introduction

There is much in the world that is artificial when it comes to a sense of community. Much that is limited by conventional thinking, much that stands in the way of discovering true community.

It is not a geographic phenomenon. It is, rather, a spiritual phenomenon. And as such, it is only genuine to the degree that one has an inner awareness of spirit.

To cultivate community therefore, one must cultivate the inner being. And when one does that sincerely, wholeheartedly, there will spring forth a garden of like-minded souls with whom one can genuinely commune.

And in this communion, this place of spiritual connection and unity, one begins to see one's outer world transformed. Indeed, one begins to see a world in which all manner of things are possible because the consciousness that the outer world reflects is itself being transformed.

This occurs to an extent on an individual level as well, when one is on a spiritual path. But when people come together with an awareness of the spirit within them and within each other, they empower one another exponentially.

That is to say they begin to bring about a world that reflects harmony and unity and grace. A world in which there is no separation, no conflict, no more exploitation of anyone or anything for personal gain. For one is living in the awareness that what one would seek from another, one already has within themselves.

Such a world may not be manifest overnight. But when people begin to come together in this way, miracles will happen. Miracles that are no more than a reflection of spiritual truth. And that truth is that we are all one.

When one is aware of this truth, separation or any sense of otherness on the basis of age or gender or race or religion or sexual preference will be seen for what it is: illusion. There will be no need to define your communities based on particular groups your ego, your small self, is willing to accept or not accept.

Instead, you will organize your communities around a sense of shared purpose. And communities will likewise be linked with other communities for a shared purpose. And so on, and so on.

And in each will be all the parts of the whole. In each will be a purpose of balancing and sustaining life in a way that extends all of life's gifts and opportunities to everyone. In each will be a purpose of contributing to the individual in equal measure to what the individual contributes. And all contributions will be recognized. Not just those that appeal to the ego sense of inadequacy or the material desires.

In this way will the world become what it has always been destined to be:a world of spirit made flesh. A world of God's design, not human design. A world in which the spirit of God within all of you is made manifest.

That this should come at a time when you have also created the means to render the planet uninhabitable by your own kind is no accident. For this is the problem, the crisis, that throws you all into a search for something beyond yourselves.

And it is this search and your participation in it, the awareness of your own soul purpose, that will guide you into real community, that will reveal your place in things—one that is perfect for each and every one of you. Perfect in ways you could never know but for the grace of God, the Great Spirit, the Universe, the Tao, the All in All.

The world is creating itself anew. And your soul has a vision of what it would give to this new world.

Discover that and you will find yourself joining with others—each with their own gifts to give—in a way that transcends borders, transcends nations and transcends human life as you know it. For such is the dream that is carried within you. And such is the opportunity at this time.

It is your choosing again. A circle within the journey in which you may yet create for eternity a garden in which all may bloom.

One

The Sole Purpose of Community Is to Serve the Soul Purpose

IT ALMOST GOES without saying that community is a way human beings can and do support each other.

But there is another dimension of community that is as important, if not more so. And that is the function of service. Serving the larger good is a dimension of community that is recognized in many communities as they are currently organized in the world.

But there is, at this time in human history, another dimension to this aspect of serving the larger good that is unfolding. And that is the evolution of consciousness and the renewal of social forms—indeed, the transformation of social and cultural structures that can no longer hold the larger vision that is being brought into the world, the paradigm shift that is occurring.

To develop this aspect of community requires an understanding of this process we are now in. And understanding this process we are now in requires an ability to perceive what is not readily apparent to anyone who has not undergone some crucial shift in their own awareness, such that they perceive what lies beyond the world of the senses.

One experiences this in many different ways. There are many paths, many teachers, many systems in practice as this expansion of consciousness is taking place. And while there is loyalty on the part of many to their particular methods and practices, and for good reason—as Joel Goldsmith put it, "No one should try to ride two horses in the same race"—there is also a great need to begin to address the questions: How does one manifest unity at every level of social organization? What are those things that have an appropriate role in any community that one would be a part of? And to what extent are we able to transcend our particular disciplines, teachings or traditions in order to manifest their essential truths of unity and conscious evolution?

If we cannot do these things, we shall be no different than those tribes that grow into nations and defend their borders of separation unto death.

Any communities we would create that will truly be able to support us and to serve the expansion of consciousness and the evolution of life on the planet will, out of necessity, need to transcend all traditional definitions. And the common link, the organizing principle, in any of them will be the purpose that is foremost within this context of conscious evolution.

So for example, one community may have as a primary focus the production and distribution of food on the planet. Another may have as its concern passing on the wisdom of the ages to all the world's children and creating opportunity for all children equally.

In communities organized in this way, in which people work together toward common goals, toward a world that works for everyone, it will matter little if one is a Christian, another a Sufi or yet another a student of Buddhist traditions or est.

This is a radical shift from the way communities have traditionally structured themselves. This is to say that, historically, community was organized around shared land, shared traditions or common racial or cultural ties. And these are the very communities that have come apart in modern technological societies.

That is because they are based on the idea of survival, and survival not for everyone, but for those few one has willingly admitted to what is called their circle or tribe or nation.

That such forms are collapsing, are being quite rapidly outgrown, is because they are based on notions that are fundamentally in error.

No community can operate at the exclusion and expense of the whole any longer. And it is the very technology on which the developed nations rely day to day that is expanding the circle to include everyone.

What has often been referred to as a "shrinking world" aspect of communications is, in reality, an expansion of one's circle, an expansion of identity to a group that now includes, or potentially includes, all of humanity.

It is for all of these reasons that the organizing principles of community must change. The organizing principles of the past, based on the superficial and the obvious will no longer do, no longer serve the growing sense of a world community, the one-world model which is the only appropriate, the only workable, the only realizable social form for the New Millennium.

Many people know this on some level. But many have had difficulty creating communities that can hold this new awareness, this new consciousness, because they were doing so only with those who shared the same religious or philosophical orientation, coastal mentality or material resources—when these are the very things to be transcended.

In other words, you are all being challenged to create community right where you are. To see that those things that link you together are manifest in your soul as a sense of purpose having to do with your particular nature and inspiration, and little to do with who you appear to be in the world.

And when you find others who are committed to this same purpose, you will, in a sense, create "virtual communities," with or without any Internet—the Internet is but a tool that reflects the deeper spiritual connections between you all. Do you see?

So, communities of people with a purpose of feeding everyone or providing educational opportunities for all or bringing the benefits of science and technology and medicine to all people of the world are going to include people from every possible background, every part of the world and every level of skill.

Purpose, soul purpose, that which you were meant to do, that which you came here for shall be the basis for communities in your one world that is emerging.

And you shall find great fulfillment in your efforts if you begin to organize yourselves in this way.

This is not to say that your role in community will be the only fulfillment in your lives, but it will be the fulfillment of an aspect of human life that has been quite lacking in the developed nations and for some time.

In other words, you will discover that, contrary to the messages of mass culture, it is not the glorification of the individual that brings a profound depth of fulfillment to life, but rather the recognition of the One Self that you all are and a devotion to, service to, a giving to this true self, a nurturing and honoring of the true self in everyone that constitutes your homecoming, your joy, your reunion, your bliss, your authenticity, your life.

To live in this awareness, to be supported in this way, will make every relationship in your life more joyful, more honest, more loving and more authentic. Indeed, this is one of the ways you will know you are in true community.

So, look to your own soul for a sense of purpose, a connection to that which is greater than any one of us, and our shared dreams, our common visions shall lead us to those of like purpose. And together, like so many pieces of a puzzle that have been scattered throughout the world, we shall come together as one, for the first time. For that is everyone's dream.

Two

Your Soul Has a Dream to Make Real

THE NOTION OF community that most people have is based on sharing at the level of what can be measured or quantified in some way. Be it land, money, food or other measurable resource.

Even in those communities where there is some measure of that which is intangible—love, peace, spirit—there are usually (but not always) restrictions or limitations on the expression of these intangible energies or qualities.

This is to say that human beings are governed to an enormous extent—far more than they are most often aware of—by a sense of limitation in all things.

This is unavoidable to some extent. For two reasons. The first is your identification with the small self. But the second, more subtle, reason is that the aspect of soul that incarnates, that chooses to express in any given lifetime, is but a holographic portion of the whole.

This is to say there is a wholeness in it, and yet there is also an awareness that it is part of something far greater to which it longs to return.

This serves you all in many ways. It serves your growing awareness. It serves healing and integration. And yet when one is not in alignment with soul, this vague longing can be misidentified as personal limitation and inadequacy, which are really aspects of ego, of small-self conditioning and separation.

In fact, until one is truly in alignment with the soul, the god self, the One Self, one will experience a continual sense of inadequacy. It is this that prompts—when the ego is seen for what it is and that is a false self—the search for another experience of life. And though the search may hold this same lesson again and again, ultimately it will become clear that the only fulfillment is in surrendering this false ego identity—a most frightening thing for most people.

That is because most people think themselves to be this false self. When this self is, in fact, comprised of what one might call "standard issue neuroses." And it is the soul self that is truly and in every way unique.

In other words, until one becomes aware of their connection to the larger whole, the soul, the being that one is that is part of the All in All that is God, that is unlimited and infinite and eternal, one cannot help but operate from some sense of, some degree of, limitation.

And limitation, whether a conscious or unconscious belief, affects all human interactions and perpetuates more of the same.

On the other hand, when one comes into an awareness that they are not what they appear to be, not mere mortals but divine creatures with magnificent souls who are here to bring into full expression that which they truly are, the whole of humanity is affected, the whole soul can be realized, the infinite capacity for abundance in all things can come forth.

It is like the tree that bears fruit unceasingly. That provides nourishment for every last one and many times over. It is the god expressing in fullness and never-ending supply.

Whenever one does this it affects the rest. Whenever two or more are in conscious awareness of this and in unity of expression, the whole is lifted. And when the whole is lifted—when all are riding the wave, new worlds are brought into being, are manifest in physical reality.

Individuals make a difference. True leaders inspire everyone. And when communities are inspired by a clarity of purpose and the soul energies of those who comprise them, there is nothing they cannot do.

And what they would do, what they would manifest is that which lies hidden, only to be discovered, at long last, in everyone. And that is to create a world that reflects divine unity, divine love, divine peace and divine appreciation and acknowledgment for everyone, every creature in the kingdom, every soul in God's domain.

Making the connection to the divine self, the soul within, is the essential prerequisite for true community, for unity of purpose, for true achievement and true power.

Until there is a critical number of individuals operating in this greater awareness in any society, harmony is not manifested at the level of the whole.

Instead, an unstable dynamic or a constant rebalancing is taking place between those individuals who appear to be in control and those who do not. And this is the phenomenon that accounts for what is called the history of the world.

At this point in human history, each one of you has seen it all. Each one of you has been on every side of the battle, experienced every aspect of the polarity. And the opportunity for union, the desire for completion and wholeness and true communion is the deeper dream within you all. *Or you wouldn't be here.*

This may come as a surprise. Or it may feel to you like something you have always, always known.

In any case, it is the way things are. Now is the moment come in which your deepest dream may be brought forth and be made real in the world.

And if you do not know the part you wish to play in this, it is time for you to discover that. For that which is within you longs to be born, longs to be expressed, longs to give your life every meaning you've ever sought, wished for, contemplated or considered.

Your whole life has been leading you to its discovery. And now the entire Universe conspires to bring it forth.

Know your heart and you will know what you are here for. And all that is meant to be yours will come to you. In order that you may give it all back to the world.

Three

Old Ideas Must Die

SPIRITUAL COMMUNITY, in reality, exists at every level. It is only in the physical world that this is not readily apparent to everyone. And that is because in the physical world very few of you know who you really are, much less who another is, in truth.

That said, we would speak to the issues that have brought you all to a point of readiness, to varying degrees—readiness for participation in the accelerated expansion of consciousness that is taking place on the planet at this time.

It is the case that most of you have not only participated in every aspect of duality and its seeming conflicts and contradictions; you have willingly chosen, at the soul level, to transcend this awareness in order to bring about a world that reflects unity.

Unity is the spiritual reality. Unity is the truth of your existence. And so unity as a manifestation of human consciousness is also a manifestation of the Divine.

When one knows this, not just as an intellectual concept but with all his or her heart, one sees everything in the world differently. One sees things the mystics have been telling us for centuries. One sees the true meaning of every teaching of every Master who has walked the earth.

And in seeing the world in this way, in this enlightened vision of the world (which is always alive, always manifest, but people do not see it), there is the most powerful presence and inspiration and peace one can ever know.

Very few will be able to sustain this experience for every moment of every day, but the smallest glimpse of this world as seen by new eyes will make everything you have ever believed about yourself or another dissolve.

You will know the truth. And, yes, it will set you free from outgrown perceptions of limitation and separation. And in this place of clarity, you will be aware of something that calls to your heart, that calls forth the gift that is uniquely you, the purpose your soul has chosen, the particular aspect of the dream that you would create.

You will know your place in the grand scheme. You will know that what you give to another is what you give to the true self that you are. You will see, as Rilke said, the god knowing itself in you. And in everyone.

And from this place of awareness and compassion and vision your authentic self will step forward to undertake the task at hand. Your soul will flow into every aspect of your life and empower you in ways you could never have imagined.

And with each one who begins to live in this way, each one who finds a calling and an answer, everyone is in greater awareness, greater light. The synergistic effect becomes greater than the mass of resistance that has permeated the predominating consciousness. And the predominating consciousness is itself transformed.

Some in the world have called this phenomenon *critical mass.* Yet there are many who have not entirely understood that it is this matter of consciousness that is the critical factor in critical mass. And not just sheer numbers of people in seeming agreement with regard to some cause or issue.

In fact, there indeed have been occasions of so-called critical-mass movements that have reflected very little expanded awareness. And this accounts for their failure.

Consciousness is the key. Intention is the key. And if your consciousness is limited by the perceptions of enemies and heroes, of good guys and bad guys, of those who are right and those who are wrong, you must do the work of opening your minds and hearts to the soul, to the truth that is within you, that enables one to transcend, to see beyond, behind and through these limited perceptions.

This is not an easy task. It requires devotion, diligence and no small amount of divine assistance (which anyone may willingly invite in at any time). But the key to expanding one's consciousness in this regard and moving to a place of clarity of intention is true humility.

This is to say that unless one holds to the truth that you and another are one, that you and another are but different expressions of the One Self, all manner of misunderstandings, misconceptions and mistakes are perpetuated in ignorance. And this is precisely what is to be transcended—the errors of limited perception.

Communities based on perceptions such as these—be they religious, secular, geographical or racial—are vulnerable to disintegration to the degree that they perpetuate these views.

Communities that are organized by self-interest on the part of a particular group and not the good of the whole will not survive.

Communities that wall themselves off from the larger community of fellow human beings make themselves vulnerable to every impulse that is moving, consciously and unconsciously, to reflect this other reality, this ultimate reality, that we are all one.

If you do not do the soul work to discover the truth of this within yourself, at the very least make this your mantra: One World, One People.

For all things which do not support this reality will fall away. And there is no small benefit in recognizing this, even if you are not entirely able to live it, to be it, to willingly participate at the highest level of awareness and authentic empowerment.

Recognize that there will be no small amount of chaos, of upheaval, as the world moves to accommodate new forms, new reflections of this greater awareness that is being born. For the degree to which you do, the degree to which you let go of resistance and allow, if not enable, this is the degree to which your personal reality will be affected, destroyed or transformed.

But recognize also the invitation that life is extending to you. Recognize also that there is in your own soul a desire for that which is occurring. And to the extent that you are able, embrace the change. And seek those communities that welcome it. It is the only way. The new world in the making is for the good of all. And anything that stands in the way of this will fall away.

Four

Paradigm Shift on a Global Scale Arises in True Community

SPIRITUAL COMMUNITY IS the only real community. While there are other artificial or apparent communities based on external connections, the connection between souls of like purpose infuses true community with the power to move mountains.

There have been and continue to be many examples of spiritual community in your midst. But it is not the prevailing method of organization. That is because most of you living in modern technologically advanced cultures are only now discovering and developing an awareness of soul and, indeed, that there is a most compelling desire within each of you that is the soul purpose, the soul dream, that which you came here for.

As this emerges—indeed, as soul purpose becomes the organizing principle for community—many of you are going to find yourselves living with a far greater sense of motivation, fulfillment, connection and true inspiration than you have ever known before.

This is to say that cooperation, not competition, will emerge as your guiding principle. This is to say that you will empower others as a way of furthering what you yourself have come here to do. This is, yes, to say that the only obstacles that you encounter to your goals will be those that refine you, clarify your process and illuminate your intent.

In other words, you will find yourself not only a part of a community, but that community will become a part of you. It will be an essential and vital and inspiring and sustaining aspect of your day-to-day life that furthers you in a way nothing else can.

Inasmuch as every community espouses these goals, there will also be a need for discernment in finding that which is truly yours. You will have to rely on your own inner wisdom to guide you in this. And you may, indeed, find that you will "try on" different groups in an attempt to discover that which is a kind of spiritual home base that supports you.

Yet when you are in true community, it will be unmistakable. It will constitute a kind of homecoming that is totally empowering. And you will recognize the other members of your group as those you have journeyed with many times before. It will feel like a part of you, this group. It will feel like a completion of some "missing" self. It will feel like your true place in the scheme of things, your second family, these kindred spirits.

This is a very powerful phenomenon. And when societies begin to be organized in this way, there will be the most amazing transformation.

Profit motives will cease to be the overriding objective of your day-to-day work in the world. Individual rights and freedoms will be seen in the context of contribution and not merely acquisition, which will have a decided impact on distribution of resources—which, is, yes, at the present time, out of balance in the extreme. In addition, what constitutes a contribution will itself be redefined, such that those things which support the community in ways previously unacknowledged or undervalued shall be appreciated and, indeed, rewarded in a manner that is consistent with every other measure of accomplishment.

These are radical notions. They are, indeed, challenges to established patterns in all areas of the culture at large. And that is the point.

When you have a society of people who are truly empowered, who know who they really are and what they are here for, the motivations, the rewards, the organizing principles, the very structures in which you operate day to day in every walk of life, every industry, every profession, every trade and every vocation will be profoundly different.

This is to say they will no longer serve the good of a few at the expense of the greater good. This is to say service will replace profit as a primary goal. This is to say furthering the evolution of the culture will be paramount and maintaining the status quo will be understood as a disservice to humanity and a form of resistance that invites destabilization and destruction of the very system one would preserve.

And so it is that spiritual community invites everyone to transform themselves and the world. And so it is that spiritual community will become the new paradigm, the central organizing principle in the so-called New Age, replacing those ethnic, religious, national and gender-based communities which have, indeed, served a purpose, but no longer serve the larger good.

They have become the special interests that impair a vision of unity, that limit the awareness of the fundamental truth that you are all one, and that you must learn to live as one in order for life to flourish on the planet—for all life even to survive the means to your demise which you have created and which is, as yet, both possible and avoidable, as it were.

It is a matter of choice for all of you. A matter of consciousness and conscience. A matter of co-creation and re-creation and living in soul awareness as much as it is humanly possible.

Because none of you do this alone, because all of you have much to give each other, spiritual community as the emerging paradigm is an essential support, an authentic requirement, a necessary vehicle for you all.

It will carry each and every one of you farther than you can travel alone. And indeed, you all have "places to go." There is much to discover in creating this new world to come.

Five

Discovering the True Self Is Discovering the One Self, the God Self You All Are

WHEN ONE IS aware of, in touch with, in connection with the divine soul within them that is the god self, their life becomes something that in many ways is not their own. This is frightening, because it challenges the ego, the identity of the small self. And the ego would have you believe that, apart from itself, nothing else exists.

And yet it is this small self that keeps the soul hidden and must be tamed, as it were, in order to serve the goals, dreams and desires of the true self. This is an ongoing process. And may well involve emotional and psychological upheaval, in order for the authentic soul self to emerge.

However, as one begins to align with the higher self—that is, bring the ego into a proper and subservient role to that of the soul self—one's outer experience is transformed in a way that reflects this internal transformation. And it is at this time that one may begin to see the divine soul self in another and another and another, that one begins to heal one's sense of separation and one's fear of one's fellow human beings.

It is this soul work, this transformational work, this process of alignment with authentic self that is a prerequisite to one's participation in true community.

For it is only in the awareness of true self that one can begin to know the soul dream, the innermost desire, the life calling that one would fulfill. And it is this soul purpose, this calling that is meant to be both shared and supported in one's true community of soul brothers and sisters who are called and devoted to the same task.

This is not to say that others in your life are not contributing and sharing with you, and you with them. It is rather the case that spiritual community is where one finds that which assists, that which empowers the life work, the outer manifestation of the unified Self.

It is when one is in the position of balance and alignment with the true self that one can be in relationship with the true self of another, the soul of another. And when two or more are in this place of authentic power, the entire Universe can move through them. The Divine can be realized, God, the Goddess, the Tao, the All in All—whatever you choose to call it, this cosmic consciousness is present and manifest and made real in the world.

> *Again I say to you, if two of you agree on earth about anything they ask, it will be done for them by my Father in heaven. For where two or three are gathered in my name, there am I in the midst of them.*
>
> Matthew 18:19-20

It is in this place of authenticity and true communion with another that one experiences the God force as transcendent or as a shared experience as well as a presence within you.

As Joel Goldsmith has said, "Separate and apart from our fellow man, there is no God to worship, no God to love and no God to serve." And, in this way, is the Divine at the center of true community.

Yet this in no way requires that you give up your individuality as so many of your fear. Or is often the case with those groups that are called cults and wherein members give their power to another in error.

Rather, in true community there is the discovery and the cultivation of that which is truly unique and that is the way in which the Divine finds expression in any individual soul. It is the soul that makes each person special, each person's contribution vital, each person's gift unlike that of any other. And it is this complete and totally unique and authentic self that everyone is seeking, unconsciously and consciously, in virtually every experience of life.

When true self is found, when it is recognized in you and in another, you will gravitate to those things which honor this Self, this purpose. Which only spiritual community can provide. And that is the sacred space to bring a new vision into the world and nurture it into existence. For that is what co-creation is.

It is the bringing forth of a shared vision. It is manifesting that which is your common purpose, your joint intention, your mutual design. And it is something you—and all people—were born to do. Though, indeed, it may take life times to really know and live in complete awareness of this divine intention.

And yet it is always evident. Often, readily apparent to others more than it is to you. Indeed, others can recognize and reinforce and help you realize that which is never entirely hidden in you, though the ego thinks otherwise, though the small self is always surprised to find this is so. And that, too, is the value of true community. It furthers the continual unfolding, the always becoming of the divine soul self that is the real you.

So when you would build a bridge to your dream, when you would satisfy your oldest, deepest longing, look not to that which is outside yourself, but all that is within.

And, as you discover that which you are called to do, meant to do, love to do, live to do, you will automatically attract and naturally encounter those who conspire (breathe together) with you. And in this conspiracy of love and support and divine intention, you will leave your mark upon the world. You will contribute that which you are here to give. You will make the angels sing for gladness, for glory in honor of what the god in you has made.

Such is the goal of everyone. Such is the journey each is on. And thus does the God force show itself in ways both eternal and new.

 Six

A New World within You Is Waiting to Be Born

WHEN ONE IS ALIGNED with soul, when one is living their soul purpose, there is a phenomenon that naturally occurs that is a most amazing and wonderful and welcome phenomenon. It is the opening of doors that were unseen or inaccessible.

This is the power of the soul. There is a magnetic force that attracts to you all that furthers what you have chosen to do through the magnetizing of the energetic field that you are. It comes to you as you are connected to—indeed, an intimate part of—the energy of the Universe and all that is God. As you live your soul purpose, as you become an expression of the Divine, as it moves in and through you, you are totally and divinely enabled.

You become the instrument, the messenger, the one who brings light, the one who is light, the one who is and always has been one with the Divine. And when you know this consciously, when you live in this awareness as much as is humanly possible, there is a divine spirit flowing through you and into the life of everyone you encounter in every moment of every day.

Of course, this is not to say you won't experience personal trials and tribulations from time to time, but you will experience them differently. You will experience them as opportunities to grow and to heal and to become ever more completely a vehicle of light, a vehicle of love, a creator of harmony and of peace.

This is the magic of transformation, the power of spirit, the sublime beauty of soulful living. It is what all are striving for and so very few know how to find. And that is because ego, small self, that which you think yourself to be, assume yourself to be, has generated every possible obstacle it could to this greater awareness for means of preserving itself, for survival against all odds.

Indeed, the path to awareness is a journey through every illusion and misconception and misunderstanding the ego has created for its own purpose. And it is this self that must give way, that must "die," that must take a back seat, if you will, in order for the soul, the god self, to be realized. And that is what all the pain of coming into awareness is really about.

It is this taming of the small self, the surrender of ego, that does not come easily. But when it comes—and, indeed, it does for everyone—this identity can be totally appreciated for what it is and was always meant to be. And that is a support, an anchor, an aspect of individuality that is so very useful in the physical world.

It is the instrument of the soul, the god self. It is the interface, if you will, between you and every other person you encounter in life. And when it is totally transparent, electrically unimpeded, as it were, there is a unity within the Self that becomes reflected in one's outer experience.

This is to say that as the Divine moves through

you in this way, it draws, it gathers, everything to you that furthers Itself. This is what more than a few of you have experienced in your most inspired moments and have come to call "getting out of your own way."

When the ego is subdued in this way, when the small self is in the service of the soul, the god self, all that one has dreamed in their heart of hearts may come to pass. All that one would give the world is brought forth in them and brought into being. All that one has chosen to do at the soul level is made manifest. Not all at once, perhaps, but increasingly and in ways that are inspiring, joyful, effortless, rewarding and fulfilling beyond measure.

This is what it is to live with authenticity, to live one's divine purpose, to live with an open heart. And it does no less than inspire everyone around you. It does no less than heal that which you devote yourself to. And that is something to be thankful for, as, indeed, the world is in need of healing. (Not to be confused with "fixing," which never lasts.) And that is precisely what each and every one of you has come here to do. To heal the world and yourselves in the process.

The particular avenue of healing that you pursue will be that which is in complete harmony with your true nature, with the manner in which your soul would express itself. And that is unique for every one of you.

So whether it is your nature to express artistically or physically, through science or as a peacemaker, or as one who heals hearts and minds, you will find yourself doing what you are uniquely suited to do, uniquely inspired to do, and therefore doing what you were born to do with love.

> *And, in the end, the love you take is equal to the love you make.*
>
> Lennon/McCartney

When you do what you love, that is its own reward. When you do what you love, anything else you achieve is secondary. When you do what you love, the entire Universe supports you in every way. And in every case, you will find doing what you love is not for yourself alone, but the fulfillment of a dream that is your gift to others.

In living your soul purpose, you live in the awareness that you and another are one. And that to serve another's highest good is to serve you own. That everything you give comes back to you. That the love you "take" is more than equal to the love you "make." It is proportional in the extreme, abundant in ways beyond measure, rich in spirit many, many times over. And what that looks like is going to be very different from one person to the next. But be assured: to live the soul purpose is to live abundantly.

So to discover one's soul, to follow the spiritual path home to the god self within, is to discover why one is here. And when one discovers why one is here and what one would give, you shall find yourself riding the horse in the direction he's going, as it's said. Your whole life will become the fulfillment of everything you ever dreamed it could be. And more.

So stay the course, whatever spiritual path you are on. Discover your own beautiful, powerful, magnificent soul. And learn what it longs to be in the world.

It will lead you to everything life has to give, everything you have to give. And, in due time, it will lead you to your soul brothers and sisters, those kindred spirits who would join their hearts and hands with yours to bring a great transformation to the planet. One in which all people live together in harmony, all people grow in wisdom, all people recognize the divine spark that is as an eternal flame within them and everyone. That, together, they are a great fire of spirit that would engulf everything and everyone in love.

For such is the ultimate reality, love is all there is.

Seven

Community Is No Mere Convention; It Is Essential

SPIRITUAL COMMUNITY AS an organizing principle in a secular culture is a radical notion. And it is impractical, if not impossible, in the minds of many.

That is because they have no connection to that which is in their own souls that would come forth. And among those of you who do, indeed, have such an awareness, there are those who have yet to discover how to live from this awareness. And, indeed, there is some fear of doing so.

There is a fear of what others will think, what others will say. There is a fear that one is, perhaps, a little bit crazy to think this way—that they have a calling, that they have a reason to be here. And there is also the underlying and greater fear of giving oneself to that which one cannot control, which is beyond the bounds of ego, of small self. A boundless divine self which you have been conditioned to deny, to repress and to contain your entire life.

It is an arduous process, this coming into soul awareness and living your soul purpose. And indeed, without a spiritual community to support this, to aid in the process and, as well, to offer guidance in the ways of the journey, the identifiable stages of the journey, few are able to find wholeness, to complete the circle of becoming that is the ever-widening arc, the ever-increasing spiral into awareness and spirit and love. (Religion does not necessarily encourage this, by the way. And that is the primary distinction between so-called religious persons and those who embark on a spiritual path.)

However, when one does have the support of such a community, be it two other people or twenty, one can move very quickly into a manifestation, an unmistakable experience of what one's particular gift is. And it is at this point that one's true community will both grow deeper and branch out.

For it is not necessary to be in the physical presence of kindred spirits to commune with them. It is not necessary to be in the same location, the same time zone or the same century. It is only a requirement that you be on the same wavelength, so to speak. And in this way can you connect and commune in spirit, in consciousness, in inspiration, in joy, in love with any soul that shares your inspiration.

In other words, to be engaged in soul work, to be at the point of living the soul dream, is to expand your consciousness beyond the space and time that your physical being resides in.

Indeed, this is a most challenging notion for the mind of the personality to accept. But it is in this way that God is always with you. It is in this way that one comes to know the true meaning of eternity. It is in this way that one is able to open up and receive the inspiration, the guidance, the support of the entire Universe and other souls within it, as one becomes the instrument of the Divine.

There is little in the way of understanding or acknowledgment of, or support for, this notion in the culture today. But there is some, and it is growing. And it is the case that the mystics and Masters have spoken of these things and more for centuries. Indeed, it is these great souls who have ascended and yet remain as the great guiding light for you all, that are available to you, accessible to you, aware of you, assisting you in your growing into a fullness of spirit, both in your first tentative expressions of soul, as well those revelations and epiphanies and ahas that can become a way of life.

This is to say that the soul is unlimited, the soul is completely tuned in, the soul is, as God is, unrestricted by the limitations of the material even as it is manifest in the material.

When one is open, when one is truly receptive to the divine energy of the soul, the god self that is an intricate and essential and purposeful part of the All in All, there is no longer an experience of separation, but only union.

In this way does unity become not merely a desire, a goal at the end of the rainbow; it becomes your reality. And when one lives in this reality, when one is aware that this is so, that we are all one, that we are all light, that we are all infinite beings, then does one see the world as it really is. And that is a place where the soul comes into awareness for its own joy.

An eye is meant to see things.
The soul is here for its own joy.
A head has one use: for loving a true love.
Legs: to run after.

Rumi*

This is bliss. This is nirvana. This is ecstasy. And it is where you will all end up eventually. It is also where you are and always have been, though you know it not, and, indeed, there is value in your forgetting.

For then your choosing to remember has power. For then it is your will to express God's will. For then and only then can you meet your Maker with an open heart as one embraces the Beloved.

Along the way, you shall meet the Beloved many times over, sometimes in recognition and awareness, sometimes not. In addition, as you climb this "stairway to heaven," as you ascend this ever-upward path, there will always, always be those who keep you from falling. And they, too, are the "arms" of the Beloved.

And this is the value of spiritual community. For not only does it empower you such that you manifest more and more of the soul dream in the physical, material dimension;it also guides you home. It lights your way. It draws you ever closer to reunion with the Divine.

* From *The Essential Rumi,* translated by Coleman Barks, with John Moyne (New York: HarperCollins Publishers, 1995), p. 107. Originally published by Threshold Books. Used by permission.

Indeed, it is the case that your membership in true community facilitates and celebrates and honors your re-membering of the Divine Self that is in you all.

This is what all Masters know, what every Master has taught. And until you have an experience of this, it may not seem at all real or even possible.

It is the role of true community to empower you even in your alternating hope and disbelief. In true community, you make the journey together, as one joins hands with another to be free.

This is the reason of the heart that reason knows not of, as Pascal said. (*Le coeur a ses raisons que la raison ne connait point.*)

Without true community it is so very easy to lose your way, to become lost, indeed, to doubt the wisdom of your own heart. Yet when hearts and hands are joined in this way, the world becomes one. As a reflection of the truth that always is. As a manifestation of divine will through each and every soul who has come here for this purpose and, ultimately, this purpose alone.

But it takes everyone to make this real for all. It is not complete, as it were, if there is even one who has gone astray. And that is why your gift is not for you alone, but always for you to give another and another and another. In this way do you know the oneness that you are.

If a man has a hundred sheep, and one of them has
gone astray, does he not leave the ninety-nine
on the hills and go in search of the one that went astray?
And if he finds it, truly, he rejoices over it more than
over the ninety-nine that never went astray.

Matthew 18: 12-13

Eight

To Find True Community, First Go Inside Yourself

THE REASON SO many of you will find much of this teaching difficult to apply and to integrate into your daily lives is that very few of you have discovered your soul purpose, your reason for being here, your gift—your unique gift—for the world. And for everyone in it.

This is something that requires a devotion to discovery, as it were. And when one is willing to explore what lies behind the dissatisfaction of the life they are living, they will discover the desire that has always been present, always a part of them.

This desire may be as a notion that has always intrigued you or it may be a well-developed vision that you have decided is impossible. In any case, once discovered, it will come as no surprise to anyone who really knows you. For, indeed, it has always influenced your expression, always colored your communication, always permeated your being.

It may be, as some would say, like water to the fish, in that it is so much a part of who you are, it has become invisible to you. And yet when you remove all sense of limitation and ask yourself what you would do, it will come forward. It will stand out in relief as that which has been the underlying essence of everything you've ever done. And it will become apparent that there are many other levels of expression for this fundamental orientation, this nature of expression, this gift that is so much a part of who you are. In other words, your soul purpose will not be at all foreign to you.

Find the thread that runs through your life, your interests, your passions, your natural inclinations and abilities, and be willing to entertain new possibilities for a fuller, richer expression of these selfsame gifts. More meaningful for you and for everyone your life touches.

That is the opportunity. That is the challenge. You needn't look to another for the answer, though indeed, others may reflect this back to you. Ask yourself, what is it that truly inspires you? Ask, what is your joy? It is, in fact, the very things you love, the very things that take you outside of yourself, outside of time and, perhaps, outside of the bounds of conventionality, the opinions and judgments of others, that are as guide posts along the way.

What is it that you can't imagine yourself not doing? What is it that has always drawn you regardless of what anyone else said or did? What is it that, even as a child, you gravitated toward, you willingly explored, you enjoyed above everything else? This is your purpose, your calling, speaking through your heart's desire.

These are the questions to ask yourself. These are the ways of finding that which is so obvious it can't always be seen. For much has been instilled in you, much has been presented to you that is, as Joseph

Campbell so often suggested, someone else's idea of what your life should be. And a good many of you have embraced this, have lived another's dream despite every disappointment. Many of you have persisted in molding yourselves to a role that doesn't fit you, which is to forsake the power and the beauty of your own soul.

This is the cost of mass culture. This is the price you pay for a society that discourages acknowledgment of and support for the ways of the soul. And yet it is never too late to bring forth that which is within you, that which *is* you, that which is your calling, your gift, your inspiration, your fulfillment and your reward.

You have only to discover this authentic self within. And there are many, many ways to do this—many teachers, many books, many paths to wisdom. They are all around you.

Pray that they reveal themselves to you and they will. Invite divine assistance in discovering your truth and expect to receive it. Indeed, it is only in making the request that this kind of invisible support can manifest, for it in all ways and at all times honors the free will of every individual. If you make such a request and are seeking with a sincere heart and an open mind, life will find a way to show yourself to you. What you see may fit no one's pictures but your own. Indeed, it may even take some getting used to on your part. But in time, you will recognize what is you. In time, you will find the courage to change your life in order to live this dream that resonates in your heart, that sparks excitement and attraction and, yes, desire deep within you.

Then and only then will you discover all that you are meant to be and become. And once you do, a new world will open up before you. And you will not be able to prevent yourself from moving toward it. Even the apparent detours will bring you closer to this dream of your soul and its coming into being in the world.

It is this dream, this soul dream, that will echo in the kindred spirits that will find their way to you and you to them. They may be right under your nose or half a world away. They may be those with whom you share little as appearances go, or those with whom you have everything in common. Indeed, they may be those with whom you have always felt a kinship, for reasons you didn't know.

This true community, this soul family that supports you, assists you and spurs you on will not be limited by any conventional definition of community. It will, rather, enable you to see that there are many different communities within your geographic community, many different communities within the business community, within any conventional community. And indeed, there are communities that transcend borders, nations, even material reality itself.

When these communities manifest (as they do in ever-increasing ways), when these new patterns of community, new paradigms of organizing, begin to gel (yes, entirely enabled by fiber-optic and satellite communications), the societies in which you live will begin to transform themselves. The cultures which comprise them will honor each other. The world in which you live and love, the world which you pass on to your children will be healed, each in time. As a task that is taken on together by you all.

As each of you move forward in this way, as each one of you realizes the Self in this way, you will empower another and another and another. And all it takes to begin it, all it takes to set in motion this journey that transforms lives, is the turning within.

Look inside your own heart. What you find there will be the fulfillment of each and every one of you. What you find there will bring fulfillment to us all.

> *If you bring forth what is within you, what you bring forth will save you. If you do not bring forth what is within you, what you do not bring forth will destroy you.*
>
> Gospel of Thomas*

* Elaine Pagels, *The Gnostic Gospels* (N. Y.: Vintage Books, 1989) p.126.

Nine

Community Is Authentic Only to the Degree that You Are

THE SOUL PURPOSE IS not the only thing you live for. There are relationships of all kinds that bring you joy and love and opportunities to learn, to come into greater conscious awareness of who you really are. But it is the soul purpose which needs to be discovered and, indeed, to be lived in order for you to feel that life has a completion and fullness and deep satisfaction that it otherwise would not have.

What is interesting is that for many of you, this fulfillment of your true vocation comes at a time when your career begins to wane or your job is outgrown. There are exceptions to this, certainly. But, for a good many of you, true vocation is something you only begin to take seriously when your other options prove so profoundly dissatisfying that body and mind begin to suffer in ways you can no longer bear.

Your capacity to continue in this way becomes reduced and then, out of necessity, you begin to examine what is in your heart of hearts. Only then do you begin to search for the "something more" in answer to the age-old question "Is that all there is?"

This is, indeed, a sad commentary on modern life. It is, in a way, a measure of how far you are from knowing your own soul, how far from the wisdom of the ages your mass cultural beliefs really are.

And it is no accident that the disintegration of this culture is now bringing the deeper questions and issues to the surface. It is no accident that more and more of you, every day, find yourselves forced to examine and to answer for yourselves the essential questions of existence which you have avoided in busyness, pursuit of ego and distractions of every kind.

It is this breakdown of that which is inauthentic at the cultural level which is allowing new solutions, new ways of being to emerge. Just as, on an individual level, it is the letting go of the old that leads to the discovery of the new. Not without pain, perhaps. But for all the right reasons.

For, in truth, no one can sustain anything inauthentic in themselves or their lives without paying the price. And that price is, for all of you, the vitality, the joy, the richness of spirit that would see you through any challenge. That would sustain and support you and, through you, inspire each and every person in your path.

There is an expression when one is in recognition of what doesn't work anymore: "My heart's not in it." And this is no mere throw-away line. It is to say that the source of your being, the part of you that is transcendent, that is bigger than the small you, the ego, that is who you really are, cannot live in this way. Yet how long you persist in this, thinking there is no other way.

This is what wears you all down. This is what brings you all such despair, such frustration, such resentment toward that which you have given so much of your life to—your reluctance to move forward, your reluctance to give it up and find another way, your fear of living your own life in a way that has no guarantees, no false sense of security to placate you, to soothe the troubled mind.

It is this quality of mind, really, that keeps you stuck. This way of thinking that is so very limited, this uninspired attitude of resignation—even cynicism—that is most in the way of your finding, discovering, that which you truly desire, that which can make you whole and complete and an inspiration to everyone.

This cynicism is pervasive. This cynicism is reinforced at every turn. And it is magnified beyond belief in the media that is central to, at the core of, mass culture. And the message you are constantly giving yourselves in your many hours a day with the black box or the flickering screen is that life is something that happens to you, something in which you are but a passive observer, rather than a powerful creator, a magnificent soul created in God's image. The message you give yourselves is that your own life is not worth living.

Does this sound extreme? Harsh? Perhaps it is. Nevertheless, this is what many of you do to yourselves day in and day out.

And it is not to say that everything that is available to you through electronic media should be condemned. It is rather to say, to make painfully clear, that this is no substitute for living your life.

If you do only those things which you think you have no choice in, those things you think you must do to survive, only to find yourself utterly exhausted and looking to some form of passive, so-called entertainment to fill you, you are suffocating your spirit. You are abandoning your soul.

And yet this is how millions of people are living their lives. This is what millions of people call progress. This is what millions of people do not see is an addiction. And the isolation that it fosters creates a continual feeling of powerlessness.

Is it any wonder, then, that when the ways of soul are presented they are often greeted with skepticism and disbelief? Is it any wonder that, for many, it takes a life crisis to bring them to a point of even beginning to honor their own souls?

It is because so very many have no experience of this, no understanding of this. So many have not felt the impulses of their own souls, the desires that stirred their own hearts to joy, since they were very young children. It may, indeed, take a devastating experience to bring you to soul awareness and the true humility that is required in the surrender of the ego to this soul self.

This is offered not merely as a grim picture of mass consciousness. It is also intended to serve anyone who is becoming aware, who is discovering their own soul and where it would take them. For, indeed, they may find that their departure from the norm may be questioned. Indeed, it may be resisted within and without. Indeed, it may not prove easy.

And yet there is everything to be gained. With even the smallest step in the direction of soul, the Universe comes forward in an embrace. With even the slightest courage, the stirring heart becomes bolder. With even a hint of willingness on your part to surrender to your soul, you will begin to see possibilities you could not before. And that is when you will find others who are engaged in soul searching. That is when you'll find opportunities and guidance along the way.

This is a journey each is on. And when one comes into the fullness and realization of one's purpose, one's gift, you will find you cannot resist your desire to share all you are learning with another. You will find that in contributing to another in this way, with an open heart and an inspired vision of all life can be, you are furthering your own experience of the same.

> *I can understand another soul only by transforming my own, as one transforms one's hand, by placing it in another's.*
>
> Gaston Bachelard
> (quoting Paul Eluard)*

* Noel Cobb, *Archetypal Imagination* (Hudson, N.Y.: Lindisfarne Press, 1992) p.94.

Know that to embark on the inward journey is to venture down the road less taken. Follow your heart and one day you will emerge as a butterfly from a cocoon, with a sense of freedom to express the divine being that you are.

Do not be too easily discouraged along the way. Do not expect those who think as you once did to cheer you on. For they may not begin to comprehend what it is you are doing.

Indeed, they may feel your actions to be a rejection of them or a judgment of all they think themselves to be. Acceptance of this on your part may make this easier on everyone, however, yourself included.

Be aware of the temptation to judge them in return, in retaliation, for anything but humility and an open heart will impede your own growth, your own discovery, your own becoming.

Instead, grant that they will, each of them, have an awakening in their own time, in their own way.

Yet in the fullness of time, you shall find yourself fulfilling your own dream and celebrating your own life. And when this time comes, there shall be no one who cannot see that this is worthwhile, that this is meaningful, that this is what they, too, would do.

And in such a way does one and another and another rise to the occasion to live abundantly. In such a way does one see that to find true community, one may give up any sense of community, of belonging—even, perhaps, of being understood by those they are closest to—only to find that this resurrection of the spirit and rebirth of the soul is the point of everything that has gone before.

This makes every heart glad. This makes every life meaningful. This makes all the difference in the world. Literally. This is how a new world comes into being through each and every one of you. It is the birth you give to yourselves.

Ten

Spiritual Community Supports Life—All Life

THE NATURE OF true self—indeed, the nature of soul—is such that one has only to let go of resistance and allow it to come forth in order to experience a life that is fuller and richer in every way, if not immediately clear in terms of direction.

This transition from living in small self to opening up to the soul is a process as opposed to an instant completion and wholeness. And it requires no small amount of trust, of faith, on your part to know that this is entirely as it should be. For until one is engaged in the process of alignment with soul and sheds much of the old patterning, one really cannot know exactly where things will lead. This not knowing is, in a sense, required. For any idea you might have of what's next for you might well be rooted in this old patterning to some degree and therefore cannot take you where you long to go in the long term.

The not knowing, the time of shedding old patterns, is an essential part of the process of truly coming into one's own. And it may prove quite challenging for the ego.

The ego has a wish to survive at all costs. And it is the breaking up of old patterns, old ways of being that do, indeed, appear as a threat to your very survival at times.

However, it is only in this way that one comes to know the authentic self, the true self. It is only in this way that the soul purpose, the life work, the dream in your heart of hearts can emerge. And once it does, you will both attract and be attracted to those with similarly inspired notions and dreams and visions.

In this way will you assist each other—sharing those dreams and visions. Asking yourselves and each other: How does one make this vision a reality? How does one bring this about? What does it mean to live from soul? And what is it that furthers my own soul that I can experience by offering this very thing to another?

For this is, indeed, how one comes into the realization of purpose. Through another, through serving another.

There is much in the culture at this time that suggests otherwise, that suggests a more self-centered approach to growth. But in truth, most of you do not think well enough of yourselves for this to be anything but a dead end. This may be conscious or unconscious. You may deny this is so. But the inadequacy of the small self that gives rise to fears and insecurities of every kind is also what requires that you do for yourself by doing for another, that you give to yourself by giving to another.

This is because of your dual nature. You are, to varying degrees, aware of soul, in touch with your authentic self and true nature at this point, but you still possess an ego. Ideally, it comes to its proper place in service of soul. But, as it yet exists, it must be reckoned with. And there is no better way to do this than to give what you would have to another. To give all you would have to another. Indeed, it is the only way.

In truth, you are one. In truth, there is no separation between you.

However, this is not to say there is no individuality. Indeed, there is a profound individuality and uniqueness in every case. And the ego is a most useful tool, a most valuable support in the expression of everything that is your uniqueness, your true self. Nonetheless, this ego also requires the willing sacrifice of anything you would have in order to truly have it, in order to feel worthy of receiving.

This is the great paradox for all human beings. And yet all you need do to understand the truth of this is to serve another in the smallest way. You will find it a most rewarding experience. Indeed, it will do more for you than anything you have ever done for yourself alone.

This is not to say that one should become a martyr or have no regard for themselves and what is appropriate for them to do in any given set of circumstances. It is, instead, meant as a clarification of the fact that when most people think they are doing what is best for themselves, it is most often the small ego self they are serving, not the true self. And in this way do they delude themselves. In this way does what may well begin as an effort to build healthy self-esteem end up reinforcing that in you which must be transcended in order to know who you really are.

The challenge and the opportunity in life is to transcend the small self.

The real you, the soul self, the god self within you, is not inadequate. It is not vulnerable. It is not dependent on anyone or anything, but completely interdependent. As well, it is autonomous of the small self. It is divine, it is the light energy of the Universe, it is beyond your ideas of what it is, as you are infinitely beyond all you think yourself to be.

Now, spiritual community, if it is genuine, is going to deepen your experience of this. Spiritual community, when it is embraced, will lead you to a greater awareness of who you really are and what this means in relationship to others. Spiritual community, when it is the real thing—and it may require no small amount of discernment on your part to know if this is really so—will further everything you ever hope to be or ever hope to do. And indeed, it will also further the shedding and the healing of all that does not serve the highest good of all.

This process will affect every area of your life. And while it may feel like you are on a roller coaster ride initially, ultimately this process will bring a more authentic quality to every relationship you have with another, be they a partner, a family member, a colleague or a stranger on the street.

Spiritual community harnesses the authentic power of souls who willingly join together to transform each of them and more. There is a synergistic effect that transcends this community and assists all others in unseen ways. There is an opening to the world soul in the collective consciousness that brings divine light to every sentient creature on the planet.

It is a most powerful phenomenon. It is a most healing phenomenon. It is a most essential—*the* most essential—aspect of bringing peace to the world, of sustaining life on the planet, of bringing forth the collective vision within your hearts and souls of all this life on earth can be.

And it is to this end that every Master supports you, every being in the angelic realm and beyond assists you. It is to this end that every one of you has a divine purpose, a unique role to play to express that within you that is one with God.

It has always been so. And yet as a new world is now in the making, it is perhaps a more compelling truth for many of you.

Love one another. Bring forth the best that is within you. Empower another and another and another to do the same. This is the purpose of true community. This is the purpose of life. You are all finding your way home together.

Eleven

Love and Light, "The Stuff Dreams Are Made Of"

As one begins to live from true self, authentic self, the soul awareness—as one begins to join with those of a similar vision and purpose and goal in their life work, a synergy is created among you to which nothing can compare.

It is this authentic power that you bring forth together that erodes the energy of established patterns, the fixed positions of old ways, the dim awareness of mass consciousness.

This is to say that there is an energetic phenomenon, an energetic effect that—though it can't yet be measured—is powerful enough to create change, to further transformation even in the most firmly entrenched aspects of any cultural or social system. And this is in addition to the wisdom that you bring to every aspect of the work itself, to any area of life you are engaged in.

This, again, is an example of both the value of each individual—individual uniqueness, purpose and perspective—and the power of like-minded individuals to create far-reaching consequences of consciousness when joined together for this purpose. Be it in person, in spirit or on line.

Conscious intention is the key. Conscious intention that is both an overriding love of life and reverence for all its forms, as well as the more specific conscious intention of any group, any community in terms of areas of healing. Areas of healing that range from healing bodies and minds to restoring and renewing the environment. From distribution of food and other essential resources to all people of the world to the dissemination of wisdom through the arts, teaching and counseling professions. From the renewal of the sacred forms and traditions—all traditions—to the renewal of the family, the extended family, the soul family that sustains you all in your day-to-day lives.

There are no limits to the possibilities. There are no natural barriers to the expression of a transformed consciousness. The only barriers, the only blocks, are man-made. Those which one encounters as resistance at both the collective and the individual level, where there is yet a total identification with the small self and the material. And this resistance, while it does not disappear overnight, need not take the form it has taken throughout so much of human history.

This is to say that extreme resistance in the form of aggression, in the form of harm to another, in the form of harm to oneself, can be disempowered, as it were. But only in a nonjudgmental awareness. Only in an atmosphere of acceptance and tolerance. Only in the light of divine truth, whether that manifests as deeds or as prayers in the hearts and minds of ordinary men and women on a daily basis. On a constant basis. At a level that becomes integrated into the emerging forms.

In other words, devotion plays a role, just as dedication does. Devotion as a time each makes in their own way to connect with the source of all within them. In this way is there a continual renewal of the strength and power and beauty of each and every soul that is creating the world anew. In this way is the god self engaged and expressed in each of you. In this way is the Divine made manifest. By whatever name you choose. (The knowing is more important than the naming.) In this way is the full and unique expression of authentic self joyful, enriching, enlivening and inspiring.

Nor is the small self, the ego, denied altogether. It is rather transformed, realigned and reinstated as the supportive vehicle it is intended to be, the transparent vessel of the soul in the physical, material world. So transparent nothing blocks the radiant light that is pouring through you into the world.

Commune with those who share your dream and this becomes a great light indeed. Share with those who, like you, have a desire to heal or inspire or reweave the social fabric, and this light becomes as a beacon guiding all from a time of being not yet born, in consciousness, to a time of awakening to all that you are in spirit and to all your world can become.

This spiritual community, this great light which guides you and sustains you, is as a reflection of the great light that you are. Each and every one. And in this light, in this state of grace and love for one another, there is no end to your discovering everything you ever hoped that life could be.

In this way do dreams come true, the dreams in every heart, the desires in every soul, the inspired visions in every one.

> *Whatever you can do or dream you can, begin it;*
> *boldness has genius, power and magic in it.*
>
> Goethe

Twelve

True Community Helps You Find Your Way Back to the Garden

SPIRITUAL COMMUNITY, true community, those communities of individuals living in and led by the ever-expanding awareness of the soul, the god self within, are those that hold the power to bring great change to the world, lasting change to the world, greater freedom and more enlightened social forms that give everyone in the world opportunities for full Self realization.

It may be difficult to grasp all the ways this may manifest or how exactly it all comes to pass. But that is the adventure, after all.

Each and every one of you is going to have a different idea of this. Each and every one of you is going to have a different purpose in this—but your ideas, your purposes, indeed, your gifts are all valued, are all essential and are, yes, all required to bring a unity of vision to that which is being born. A unity of vision that is large enough to grant an appreciation for all people, a sustainability for all life, a viable, and yet totally inspired way of honoring what each of you has come here both to accomplish and to give.

Only in this way can the One World, One People that you are manifest in all the ways that it must in order for life to continue on the planet. In order for you all to live in conscious awareness of that which you create and co-create, that which is for the good of all people, all life, as opposed to that which is limited and therefore cannot endure.

This is to say that if you grow into awareness of true self, if you participate in what is called true community, you cannot help but see yourself in another and another and another. You cannot help but see that you are all one. And that your dream to live in peace, your dream to love one another, your dream to experience joy in all things is not yours alone.

And that is because the true self that you are is the God force, the Divine, yet another facet of the All in All, a precious and unique expression of the Great Spirit that is in all things.

> *When I began to own my own soul life, I also began to see that it wasn't only mine. There was another dimension which didn't really belong to me. What freedom! To discover that I was also Everyman, Everywoman! The same currents of soul flowing through me as the person walking beside me. We meet in this river—not the petty personal one in which so many schools of psychology get caught—but the bigger one, the greater river.*
>
> Noel Cobb*

This is the realization human beings are coming to in this time. This is the unity consciousness of which so many speak, that so many are presenting as the new paradigm for the New Millennium. And,

* Noel Cobb, *Archetypal Imagination* (Hudson, N. Y.: Lindisfarne Press, 1992) p. 52.

indeed, they are correct.

Yet if you do not experience the reality of this, if their words are just words, if you do not have ears to hear, these dreams cannot be made real, made manifest.

To bring forth a vision for all of humankind, to create a new world in which the truth of the spirit is made manifest, the truth of the spirit, the soul, must be real for everyone.

This is what transformation is all about. To transform is to transcend one's sense of separation and isolation and desperation and experience the illusion of these things. To experience the illusion of these things, one must experience what is real or else the illusions persist as the only "reality" one knows.

In other words, spiritual community is the way in which the world of illusion is transformed and transcended. True community brings you to the deeper truth in yourself and another. Authentic community—that based on the reality of the soul and not geography or gender or genetic lines—is the way in which you experience what it is to live from this truth of who you really are. And in that experience you discover the ways and means to bring this truth to a wider and wider circle of fellow human beings.

However, if there is any limitation in this you will come up against it in another. And your opportunity will be to expand your truth. If there is a clash between circles, a discrepancy from the perceptions of one community to the next, see it as an opportunity to learn from one another in an ever-increasing awareness. And if there is any conflict within your communities, likewise allow this to be a refinement process, one in which an open sharing of differences leads you all to yet more expanded truth.

Truth will not lead you to sameness but to appreciation. Awareness will not lead you to deny another's freedom but to encourage it. Love will not lead you to the glorification of any individual but to a sense of awe and reverence and gratitude for the infinite and profound expression of the One Self that dwells within you all.

This is the great mystery of life—the ways in which you are all coming to discover the divine that is within you and in everyone.

True community facilitates that. True community nurtures that. True community allows you to express that, experience that and share it in ways that make every part of life a reflection of divine truth.

In this way does one experience the heaven that is on earth, which otherwise one does not see. In this way does one see every exchange with another as a meeting with the Divine. In this way does one come to know the truth of who one really is and the truth of the One Self that is God. By whatever name you choose.

No more shall you wander in search of what has always been within you. No more shall you deny that which is also in another and in everyone. No more shall you suffer the limitations you have continually created for yourself in order to discover the magnificence of your true being.

And when people of the earth come together in this way, in all the splendor of the authentic and true nature, you shall, again, find yourselves in the garden. For no other reason than to experience joy, embrace love and give all infinite expressions of these to one another.

This is what life on earth can be. A profoundly beautiful expression of the All in All, the Infinite Divine that has no beginning and no end.

This earthly life is but one circle in a creation that is beyond your imagining. Yet it is no less exquisite or essential than any other. And, as circles within this circle of the garden, your communion—for that is what true community really is—shall help you all, each one of you, find your way home at last.

The drunkards are rolling in slowly, those who hold to wine
are approaching.
The lovers come, singing, from the garden, the ones with
brilliant eyes.

The I-don't-want-to-lives are leaving, and the I-want-to-lives
are arriving.
They have gold sewn into their clothes, sewn in for those who
have none.

Those with ribs showing who have been grazing in the old
pasture of love
are turning up fat and frisky.

The souls of pure teachers are arriving like rays of sunlight
from so far up to the ground-huggers.

How marvelous is that garden, where apples and pears,
both for the sake of the two Marys,
are arriving even in winter.

Those apples grow from the Gift, and sink back into the Gift.
It must be that they are coming from the garden to the garden.

*Rumi**

* "The Drunkards," a Rumi poem, translated by Robert Bly, from *News of the Universe: Poems of Twofold Consciousness,* edited by Robert Bly.